Resilience Ready™

THE LEADER'S GUIDE TO THRIVING THROUGH UNRELENTING CRISES

Vivian Blade

Ignite Press
Fresno, CA

Published in the United States by Ignite Press.
ignitepress.us

ISBN: 978-1-950710-99-7 (Amazon Print)
ISBN: 978-1-953655-00-4 (IngramSpark) PAPERBACK
ISBN: 978-1-953655-01-1 (IngramSpark) HARDCOVER
ISBN: 978-1-953655-02-8 (Smashwords)

For bulk purchase or booking, contact:

Vivian Blade
vivian@vivianblade.com

Library of Congress Control Number: 2020918913

Cover design by Salman Sarwar
Edited by Chris Karmiol

OTHER BOOKS BY VIVIAN BLADE

FuelForward: Discover Proven Practices to Fuel Your Career Forward

Acknowledgements

I want to use this opportunity to express my gratitude to several people who helped make *Resilience Ready* possible.

My greatest appreciation goes to my husband, Vance Blade, the love of my life. You have always supported me in any endeavor and have been an inspiration in my life. You shared ideas, experiences, and encouragement throughout the process of writing this book. You are the role model of a Resilience Ready Leader, both in your personal and professional life. God fulfills His purpose in your life as you persevere in service and encouragement to others. You are a man of integrity and faith, who makes a huge difference in the lives of your family, friends, and colleagues. I am so blessed that God has given us this life to experience together. For you, I am eternally grateful.

I also am grateful to my parents (the late) Elbert and Zada Stowe Hairston, who instilled in each of your seven children a strong foundation for resilience. You raised us in an environment of love, positive perspective, hope, and Christian faith. We watched you persevere as you moved through life's challenges and fulfilled a meaningful purpose in service to others. You taught us how to stand for what is right and honorable. You pushed us to take on leadership roles, and to be involved in activities that made us stretch and grow. You inspired resilience by introducing us to scriptures, such as Psalm 23, Luke 6:28, and Philippians 4:13; to songs, like "The Impossible Dream" and "Climb Every Mountain"; and to poems, most notably, "Invictus." Those experiences were crucial in shaping who we are today, and we are privileged to live out your legacy, and to pass it on.

A special thank you to the leaders who so willingly shared your time, experiences, and lessons learned for this book: John Hackett, Elizabeth

Hill, Tonya Jackson, Dr. Todd Mooradian, Carmen Moreno-Rivera, Nackia Salmon, Vicky Stevens, and Andrea Towns. Your stories will be an inspiration to others.

I am especially indebted to those who invested their time and focused effort to provide early feedback on the manuscript: Vicky Stevens, John Hackett, Larry McDonald, Elizabeth Hill, Raymond Gazaway, Cathy Fyock, and Alfonso Cornish. Your insights helped make this an even richer body of work. Cathy Fyock also served as my book coach, sharing strategies and ideas, as well as motivation to be resilient when the writing process got tough.

Thank you to my siblings, friends, and colleagues who shared your ideas, feedback, and inspiration throughout this book project.

I am ever so grateful for the ongoing support and inspiration from our beautiful, talented children, Alivia and Percy, his wife Danitsa, and our new grandson, Novak. We are so proud of who you are, all you have accomplished, and the resilience you have grown into in your lives!

Finally, I thank God for this opportunity and for His eternal blessings in my life.

Table of Contents

Introduction

I was working at my desk one morning when the phone rang. I answered the phone, and my human resources manager was on the other end of the line. I had gotten "the call." I was being laid off from a nearly thirteen-year career with one of the world's most respected companies. I was moving up in my career, had given so much in my years with the company, and had a bright future in leadership ahead. What did this mean for my career? How would I help support our family? How could this be happening to me?

The company had been through a couple of rounds of layoffs by this point. So, though this didn't come as a total surprise, still, it hit hard and felt very personal. I had to remind myself that it was *not* personal, that I still had value, and these are hard business decisions that are not easy for anyone to make.

It had been a tough six months prior to my being laid off. My department was being eliminated, and my team had been realigned with other functions during the division's reorganization. Like many other leaders, I only had a few weeks to either find roles for my team elsewhere across the company, or lay them off. Grim economic conditions were putting pressure on operating results for the foreseeable future. If things didn't improve, more layoffs would be imminent.

Employee morale was understandably down, and the rumor mill up. As a leader, I had to figure out how to support my team and work with other leaders to get our company through this crisis. In a few short weeks, the cuts went deeper. I was faced with having to lay off some members of my team. Not only is that a painful message to receive, it's also tough to deliver.

Though this was a very emotional time, looking back I could see how God instilled in me a capacity to recover quickly from difficulties, and how my faith provided a foundation for the uncertainty I was about to face. I was out of town on business when rumors of potential layoffs began circulating.

While traveling, close family friends, the Hoskins, invited me to attend a revival at their church. The evangelist, gospel artist Marvin Sapp, spoke from 2 Chronicles 20. In this book of the Bible, King Jehoshaphat, a faithful leader of the country of Judah, and his people were warned that vast, more powerful armies were planning to wage war against them. They came together to ask God to help them through their crisis.

It struck me that God's response to the people of Judah in their state of uncertainty, anxiety, and fear offered a message that paralleled my own circumstance. God's message inspired hope, brought calmness, and strengthened their faith: [15]"Do not be afraid or discouraged because of this vast army. For the battle is not yours, but God's. [17]You will not have to fight this battle. Take up your positions, stand firm and see the deliverance the Lord will give you. Do not be afraid; do not be discouraged. Go out to face them tomorrow, and the Lord will be with you." 2 Chron 20: 15, 17

It was not a coincidence that I had gone on that business trip and attended the service that evening. I felt as if this message was given to me to share with my team members and others who were anxious about the state of our business and potential layoffs.

As I worked with my colleagues through this crisis, and as my layoff eventually transpired, I realized this message of hope was also for me. It gave me the confidence that I was not alone in this battle, and that, with God, the situation was going to work out OK. The road would not be easy, and the journey forward would at times come with its share of disappointments. But if I kept the faith, kept moving forward, and sought strength in God, He would be fighting this battle, opening doors, and making a way even when I didn't realize it.

God had prepared me for this time in more ways than I realized. I had been blessed with vast career, business, and leadership experience with the world's top Fortune 100 companies. Although the results of an outplacement career survey suggested that entrepreneurship might not be the best career direction for me, after consideration and prayer I discovered that my purpose was to use my leadership expertise to help other professionals and organizations succeed. I had to lean on my faith and find the courage to forge ahead toward starting my own business in the midst of an economic downturn.

Why You Should Read This Book

Learning from Experience

As I have grown in my career in various leadership roles, I've endured my share of challenges. I can recall a number of times when I've tried to look calm, cool, and collected on the outside, but didn't feel quite that way on the inside. Experiences like the personal crisis I shared above taught me a lot about how to move beyond simply surviving through such situations.

I've discovered how resilience is crucial to getting through a crisis without it absorbing your psychological, emotional, spiritual, physical, or financial well-being. I've learned about the critical role leaders play in how their teams and organizations navigate through crises, and how not only your operations, but, more importantly, your people can make it through even the toughest circumstances.

Times of challenge and crisis call on us to be resilient in order to remain courageous and encourage others through the struggle. In this book, I will share what I have learned along the way about resilience, and how the resilience principles I introduce transformed the path for leaders and organizations I've worked with in my practice, leaders I interviewed for this book, and myself.

A Leadership Crisis

As a leadership and organizational development expert, I work with organizations to grow their talent into inclusive servant leaders equipped to steer their teams through all sorts of challenges.

From my considerable experience working with global and regional organizations, I can tell you that we are not only fighting the health, societal, and economic crises that arise, we also are fighting a leadership crisis that should concern you.

I often see leaders struggling with how to get their organizations through the day-to-day crises they face. They severely lack the skill of resilience. Stress causes some leaders to believe they have to prove their toughness. They are needlessly hard on their employees. They put on armor, ready for battle, even with the people who are there to support them. Other leaders acquiesce. They are so fearful of making mistakes — often the result of their organizational culture — that they fall victim to the crisis, or settle for the conditions in which they find themselves.

Organizations with these types of leaders can't survive a crisis. Sure, the crisis will eventually pass. But ineffective leadership will cause an organization to be crippled with dysfunction, disengaged employees, suffering productivity, and dismal operational performance.

The Call for Resilience

What organizations need are resilient servant leaders, equipped to build an even stronger sense of community across the organization, putting it in a position to once again thrive. Resilient leaders inspire resilient teams and resilient organizations.

Resilience is not an achieved state of enduring existence. You don't arrive at a level of resilience with a protective shield forever surrounding you. Resilience is a learned skill based on a set of principles and practices developed over time. Adversity comes in all shapes and forms. Every crisis has unique characteristics and challenges that will stretch you in different ways. As you become more skilled at the practice of resilient leadership, you become *resilience ready*, better able to adapt to and persevere through the demands you'll face.

Resilience is an ongoing journey. Becoming skilled at resilience requires your commitment to learning and working at the principles when you are *not* in a crisis. Your muscle memory must be able to kick in as crises confront you.

This Book Is for You If...

You are *in the middle* of a crisis right now, and...

- Stress from the uncertainty and fear are threatening your well-being.
- Stress from uncertainty and demanding workloads are threatening the well-being of your team and organization.
- You are struggling to be the resilient leader your team needs.
- Your leadership approach to the crisis is void of humanity. You struggle with how to connect to and support your team.
- You are constantly worried and distressed about the crisis.
- You feel like you, your team, and/or your organization are stuck figuring out how to get through the crisis in one piece (and don't know how to get unstuck).

You are *not* in a crisis right now, and...

- You want to reflect on your resilience during a recent crisis, identifying where you might need extra attention.
- You know resilience was missing in your leadership during a recent crisis and there were negative outcomes that you don't want to repeat.
- You want to make sure you're ready for the next crisis around the corner.

- You need to ensure the leadership teams within your organization are prepared to lead with resilience as future crises emerge.
- You need to strengthen your leadership development programs by integrating the resilient leadership principles in this book.
- You are aware that resiliency is a critical skill to build across your organization.

Resilience Ready™: A Leadership Framework

Resilience Ready reveals a framework for how these principles have helped me and other leaders get through the greatest challenges of our generation.

This book does *not* teach you the nuts and bolts of creating or implementing an operational crisis or disaster recovery plan. *Resilience Ready* guides you in how to build your personal resilience skill, so you are equipped and ready to lead with the resilience your team needs. These resilience principles integrate with servant leadership principles so that stronger, more humane leaders and organizations emerge.

Servant leadership flips the traditional organizational hierarchy and considers employees, rather than leaders, as most important. It doesn't mean that leaders give up their power, but emphasizes *power with*. The relationship becomes a partnership. Servant leaders genuinely care about the growth and well-being of others. They want the best for their team and create an environment where individuals are valued, empowered, growing, and contributing at their highest levels. Because of the intense nature of a crisis, and the stress it places on an organization, leaders must be genuinely attentive to the impact on and well-being of their teams, customers, partners, and communities. Resilience is an integral part of the ability to fulfill this crucial leadership role.

Resilience Ready begins by revealing in Part 1 the crisis we face with leaders who are ill-equipped to lead their organizations through adversity, which we will continue to experience at a more rapid pace than ever before. I discuss the impact and the contributors to this resilient leadership crisis.

Part 2 of this book introduces the solution to this leadership crisis, the Resilience Ready Leader's Guide. This guide lays out a framework for building leadership talent capable of steering your organization through even the most extreme adverse situations with resilience. The roadmap begins with developing your personal resilience skill around a set of essential resilience principles. These principles and associated servant leadership practices give you a foundation and toolkit for growing resilience across your teams and within your organizational culture.

If you could use support in getting yourself and/or your organization resilience ready, don't hesitate to contact me at vivian@vivianblade.com.

It's time to lead with resilience!

Meet the Leaders Featured in *Resilience Ready*

To prepare for this book, I held a series of interviews and discussions with prominent leaders. They have graciously shared their resilience leadership experiences, perspectives, lessons learned, and best practices.

Meet the leaders featured throughout this book:

John Hackett

John Hackett is the former president of the Midsouth Division of the Kroger Co. He served as president for 24 of his 50 years with the company before retiring.

As the Midsouth president, he was responsible for 163 stores in the states of Kentucky, Tennessee, Indiana, and Illinois. He supervised Kroger's retail stores, pharmacies, and fuel stations. His division employed 22,000 associates. He currently serves on the Board of Directors of The Kentucky Retail Federation and Dare to Care Food Bank. He is a former member of the Board of Trustees at Bellarmine University, the Board of Overseers at the University of Louisville, and the Louisville Urban League.

Elizabeth Hill

Elizabeth Hill, MA, Family and Consumer Resources, Infant and Child Development focus, has worked in the field of early childhood development and education for more than 30 years, where she is recognized as a creator of effective early childhood programs and a champion of its leaders. She has made countless contributions to the field, working in classrooms and administration, regulatory and quality assessment, and professional development, as well as designing and instructing college courses and programs. Prior to her current role as a mentor, coach, and consultant, she served as program director of the Early Childhood Development Program in the Division of Arts and Sciences at Florence-Darlington Technical College. Through her visionary leadership, Ms. Hill established an academically strong program through a relationship-based approach dedicated to promoting respect and resilience among students.

Tonya Jackson

Tonya Jackson is the Senior Vice President, Chief Supply Chain Officer for Lexmark International. She is responsible for worldwide supply chain strategy and operations, including demand/supply planning, global sourcing, hardware and supplies manufacturing, distribution and logistics, shared services, and corporate real estate strategy and management. Ms. Jackson is a strong, well-rounded leader with more than 25 years' experience in high-tech operations and research & development, including a stint with IBM. Her depth of cross-functional knowledge enables her to relate to people and positively lead organizations through significant, often difficult change. She is known for her adaptability, her passion to build strong teams through mentoring and development, and for her collaborative and open approach that drives engagement, communication, commitment, and success.

Dr. Todd Mooradian

Todd Mooradian Ph.D. is the Dean of the University of Louisville College of Business. Before joining the University of Louisville, Dr. Mooradian spent 27 years at the College of William and Mary in Virginia where he was the Associate Dean for Faculty and Academic Affairs and the William J. Fields Professor of Business at the College of William & Mary Mason School of Business Administration. Dr. Mooradian is an expert in marketing strategy and consumer behavior. Much of his research focuses on the psychology behind consumer satisfaction, loyalty, and branding. He has also published two books and over 20 chapters and articles in academic journals including the *Journal of the American Marketing Society*, *Management Learning*, *the Journal of Business Strategy*, and *the Journal of Economic Psychology*.

Carmen Moreno-Rivera

Carmen Moreno-Rivera is the Chief of Performance Improvement for the Louisville Metro Government in Louisville, KY. Prior to joining the public sector, Carmen applied her engineering expertise in private industry as she advanced in leadership with United Parcel Service, a top global brand. As a visionary change leader, she is dedicated to driving continuous improvement. Progressive and solution-orientated, she is known for creating business value and leading organizational change through challenging times.

Nackia Salmon

Nackia Salmon is the Aviation Services Cost Data Strategy Leader for GE Aviation. She is as a high-energy, strategic thinker who utilizes Operational Excellence and Lean Six Sigma know-how to connect with teams and rewire processes and mindset to execute on business goals in complex environments. Her career has spanned IT leadership roles in Fortune 500 companies such as GE and Ryder System, Inc. Her passion project is My Story, an organization she founded which helps people deal with feelings of being stuck in their lives by sharing their stories with others.

Vicky Stevens

Vicky Stevens has been a human development professional for over 28 years in the for-profit and nonprofit sectors. She's had a varied career, having worked as a faculty member and career services director in higher education, an entrepreneur, a consultant, and a professional in the areas of organization development, talent and leader development, curriculum design, assessment feedback, and employee well-being. She believes that resilience is at the core of employee engagement and workplace satisfaction, and she strives to make those around her feel encouraged, supported, and provided with the resources to succeed in the workplace.

Andrea Towns

Andrea Towns is the Vice President of Finance Operations and Technology for a Fortune 500 financial services company. She has experience as a world-class senior leader with long-term success as a business driver, finance expert, FP&A leader, and change agent in cross-cultural environments with Fortune 500 companies Mastercard, Baker Hughes, and GE. She has an extensive track record in building and directing high-performing finance organizations through major transitions and growth initiatives.

How to Use This Book

Resilience represents your capacity to persevere through life's toughest challenges. Resilience positions you to be in control of your crisis response. With resilience, you don't let a crisis defeat you, nor do you become victimized by it, riding it out or skating through until it's over.

Resilience is a learned skill based on a set of principles and practices developed over time. Developing your personal resilience skill and leadership resilience skill requires awareness, intention, and commitment to the ongoing work prior to and during a crisis.

A basketball player must have a ball inflated with the right amount of air for it to have the proper bounce, or to pass well. But the ball doesn't bounce or pass by itself. Playing the game well requires the basketball player to develop her skill at the game by learning, conditioning, practicing, and working with her coach and team.

To become effective at leading with resilience requires you to develop your skill by learning, conditioning, practicing, and working with your coach and team.

To get the most from this book, I recommend the following approach:

Inspiring Personal Resilience

- *Grasp the principles* — This book takes you in depth through each of the five Resilience Ready Principles. Read, study, review, and understand the principles and associated leadership practices.

- *Identify and address the obstacles to becoming Resilience Ready* — You have to know where you currently stand in order to map out a path to change. Identify and prioritize the specific obstacles that need to be addressed to begin deepening your personal resilience skill. Complete the Resilience Ready Self-Assessment to identify where you are in your resilience readiness and any contributing factors. Get feedback from your team and others who are familiar with your leadership by having them complete the Resilience Ready Feedback Survey.
- *Take action toward becoming Resilience Ready* — Everyone is different, and your experience and needs during a crisis will vary. Discover areas among the five Resilience Ready Principles that would help strengthen your resilience right now. Utilize the reflections, recommended actions, and resources that accompany this book to enhance your skill across the Resilience Ready Principles. Engage a mentor or executive coach to help you explore ideas and keep you accountable.
- *Practice the Resilience Ready Principles* — Identify opportunities to integrate the Resilience Ready Principles into your life and leadership practice. Align your practice of these principles with your needs, values, personality, and leadership style. Be intentional about putting the principles and strategies into practice without expecting everything to go perfectly.
- *Reflect and adjust* — Reflect on the outcomes of your practice. Were the results what you expected? What would you repeat or do differently next time? Retake the self-assessment to see how your resilience readiness has evolved. Commit to ongoing learning, development, and practice.

Inspiring Team Resilience

As you build your personal resilience skill, you will be able to support and encourage others in building theirs.

1. Be a role model. Lead by the example you would be proud to have others follow.
2. Provide training and support, and create a culture that helps employees build and practice their resilience skills. Integrate

the steps outlined above, "Inspiring Personal Resilience," to get the most out of this book.

3. Gather with your team to complete the "Inspiring Team Resilience" exercises for each principle that you'll find in the *Resilience Ready Leader's Guide* workbook.

Inspiring Organizational Resilience

1. Identify and prioritize obstacles to begin building Resilience Ready Leaders, Resilience Ready Teams, and a Resilience Ready Organization. Design a leadership development training program based on the Resilience Ready Principles that address the specific needs of your organization.
2. Align these resilience principles with the values and competencies important to your organization's success. Define associated behaviors that integrate the principles into the organizational culture.

Action is the key. If you're in the middle of a crisis now, you need to build resilience skills quickly to weather the storm.

The next crisis is right around the corner. Will you be ready? This book is your roadmap to get there.

So, let's get started!

PART 1

THE LEADERSHIP CRISIS

Chapter 1

The Leadership Crisis

Crisis — The Uninvited Visitor

You've seen it in the eyes of the people around you. You've felt it yourself... the panic that sets in as a crisis hits.

The Global Financial Crisis. The Great Recession. The COVID-19 pandemic. September 11 terrorist attacks. The Great Depression. The dotcom bubble. Hurricanes. Tsunamis. Wildfires. E. coli contamination. Competitive threats. Mergers and acquisitions. Product recalls. Employee union strikes. Equipment failures. Leadership ethics or mismanagement issues. Supply chain problems. Financial forecast misses. Cyber security breaches. Massive layoffs. You... laid off. Personal or family illness. Broken friendships. Eviction notice.

These are just a few of the most visible examples.

Crises cause significant impact to economies, companies, and individual lives. How many crises have had an impact in some way on your company? On you personally?

You know a crisis will eventually hit your organization. Some are unanticipated. Some you forecast as part of risk management planning. You can't pinpoint exactly what or when or how the next crisis will appear, and you don't often get advance notice.

A crisis doesn't have to be a broad national or global emergency. Every day organizations experience challenges that impact their financial and industry well-being, the well-being of their employees, and that of their customers. A supplier can't ship parts. A major storm shuts down airports and highways. An executive commits an integrity violation that damages trust. A security breach has taken down your systems, bringing operations to a standstill. A fire shuts down production for months. The unanticipated complexity of a merger or acquisition reduces ROI. A labor shortage impacts your ability to meet customer demand. Regulatory changes negatively impact your company and industry. Sales declines prompt cost reduction measures.

How well are you dealing with these types of ongoing disruptions?

Your disaster response planning must consider your approach to leading the human capital side of a crisis, a resilience approach. #ResilienceReady

---

Even if you have a risk management plan for anticipated crises, there are unknowns. You are writing parts of the playbook as you go. "Everything looks like it's on fire during a crisis, and you can get distracted," warns Tonya Jackson, SVP, Chief Supply Chain Officer for Lexmark International. "There's a lot of things that you could do, but you have to figure out what you should do."

Your disaster response planning must go beyond the steps to address the operational issues to include considering your approach to leading the human capital side of a crisis, a resilience approach. Resilience enables you to lead with a calm, thoughtful demeanor, rather than an anxious, potentially reckless one. As a Resilience Ready Leader, you are equipped to overcome the overwhelm, recover quickly, and get faster results.

The New Reality

It seems like we barely get past a crisis when the next one emerges. Multiple crises like those mentioned above even overlap each other. PricewaterhouseCoopers (PwC) found, in their Global Crisis Survey 2019, among senior executives who had experienced a crisis that "regardless of the nature of that initial crisis, nearly half (47%) suffered an ancillary crisis that was operational in nature." Futurists predict that in the next 10 years we will experience more frequent crises.

We have increasingly become a global society. The challenges facing one part of the world will, in some way, shape, or form, impact other parts of the world. The supply chains of various industries are interconnected, so the challenges facing one industry will affect many others. The speed of change in technology advances, and the competitive environment in which your company operates makes your organization susceptible to increased ongoing risk of major operational disruption, challenge, and crisis.

As a Resilience Ready Leader, you are equipped to overcome the overwhelm, recover quickly, and get faster results. #ResilienceReady

The challenge for government and industry is less about being ready for large-scale crises to hit, and more about being consistently ready for the problems and disruptions that will inevitably arise.

While you may expect large-scale crises to catch you off guard, the inability to face ongoing challenges potentially poses even greater risk. It's true that a significant crisis brings about significant change. However, change is constantly surfacing from the day-to-day challenges that emerge. Your best position is to be ahead of change, proactively creating and influencing, rather than reacting to it.

Consider This

What crises have you faced over the past 12 months? Which were of global or national scale? Which were of industry scale? Which were of business scale? What has been the impact on your organization from each? What has been the impact on you personally?

Your Leadership Crisis

When I worked for GE, the company adjusted leadership tenures from two- to three-year terms to three- to five-year terms. Part of the rationale was to allow leaders to experience and lead through the results of decisions they made early in their roles. Secondly, a longer tenure in a role would allow leaders to experience different business cycles — the ups and downs. This extended role tenure would serve as a test of a leader's effectiveness and potential.

Leading through a crisis requires a calm, steady hand, solid competence in skill, agility in strategy as the winds shift, and a strong will to survive. #ResilienceReady

Your mission leading through a crisis or business challenge is to discover and capitalize on the upside, and come out with minimal damage to the business. How do you keep the business afloat and be well positioned to return to growth?

When business is going well, ideally with double digit growth (or at a minimum above GDP), it can be easy to coast along like a sailboat on the ocean, gliding almost effortlessly with the calm winds. Leading through a crisis, like navigating a sailboat through a storm, is an entirely different challenge. It requires a calm, steady hand, solid competence in skill, agility in strategy as the winds shift, and a strong will to survive. Weathering the storm requires strong resilience. Remarkably, this level of resilient crisis leadership is largely absent in most organizations.

The leadership crisis that demands immediate attention: *Leaders are not prepared for the unrelenting crises that are more prevalent and emerging more rapidly.*

In a corporate board survey on crisis preparedness, Deloitte found that "only 49% [of respondents] say their companies have playbooks for likely crisis scenarios. Even fewer (32%) say their companies engage in crisis simulations or training...It's noteworthy that almost one-fifth of board members say they have no crisis playbook. But it may be more telling that one-third [of board members] don't even know if they have one."

How many leaders in your organization are truly prepared to weather these frequent storms? How many can do so with resilience? What about you? Do you find yourself often struggling in a crisis? You end up struggling to keep your head above water, thrown into survival mode without a lifejacket, rather than having the preparedness and resilience to skillfully sail your way through the turbulence. Admittedly, you question yourself. Your past experiences may have been quite difficult, and the outcomes were not as you hoped.

The leadership crisis that demands immediate attention: Leaders are not prepared for the unrelenting crises that are more prevalent and emerging more rapidly. #ResilienceReady

During times of crisis, the weight on leaders' shoulders can be overwhelming. The situation changes rapidly. You don't have all the information you need to make the most informed decisions. The uncertainty makes employees anxious. Pessimism, due to a lack of control, quickly sets in. Pandemonium can take hold if leaders don't lead with resilience.

How you lead through these times will dictate not only the health of your operations, but, more importantly, the health and commitment of your employees, customers, and other partners.

Thrown into a Tailspin

Just like the widespread layoffs my company faced during the economic downturn, when tough times hit, future uncertainty generates great anxiety. You're left with countless questions about how to get through this, and even forced to make some critical, potentially life-altering decisions. You may have to act quickly and decisively, even in the face of uncertainty. You're nervous. You don't want to make the wrong decisions, which often carry substantial impact. Many people can be affected, and a lot is at risk. You question your decisions, and multiple "what-ifs" resonate in your mind. The pressure is on!

PwC's Global Crisis study also reveals that "the reality, unfortunately, is that when an actual crisis hits, 'corporate crisis response' and 'corporate values' often appear to go in separate directions."

These crises can put you in a state of what feels like constant chaos. There is so much going on in your head, so many directions you could go, you feel like you're everywhere all at once. Sometimes you feel like your hair's on fire. You just need the chaos to stop, and for your thoughts and actions to come together with clarity. You may get to a point where you see connections beginning to form, but you don't have a solid path to the solution. You feel like you will fall into a dark hole if the chaos continues.

The overwhelming stress of the situation and inability to control what happens, or the outcome, can paralyze you. Especially early on, the darkness of the situation prevails. You can't yet see a way through it all. The wall feels too thick to break through and too high to climb over. There's no visible light at the end of the tunnel.

Emotions Run High

When a failed systems integration causes an inability to access information to service customers from the front lines, you've got a serious crisis on your hands. Emotions run high. Customers are calling and complaining. Employees are idle or reverting to manual, inefficient processes. Everyone scrambles trying to find and fix the problems. People tend to point fingers and find scapegoats.

Just thinking about similar experiences causes your body to tense up. You can feel the stress. Because of the uncertainty, pressure, fear, and heightened sensitivity that emerge during these challenges, it's easy to react from a place of pure emotion, which could lead to trouble. You tend to not be your most rational self when emotions are high. Your primitive amygdala brain kicks in with an automatic response to protect you, launching an amygdala hijack, a response intended to sense danger and generate an impulse reaction to keep you from harm. That may not be the best response.

Emotion during times of challenge and stress is not all bad. It can help keep you from becoming complacent. You need high emotion to create the necessary adrenaline to make a move.

PwC concludes from senior executives' responses to their Global Crisis Survey that "emotions are extremely powerful — and that the experience of crisis will alter the chemical balance of human behavior (including in your network of stakeholders) in ways that are impossible to predict. Successful companies know that no amount of systems, data, or software will help you manage a crisis effectively if your people don't step up to the plate."

The key is to recognize the emotion and stress building inside, and, instead of responding immediately, process the emotion and what it is driving you to do. *Where does that emotion show up, how does it show up, and how does emotion manifest itself in my leadership practice?*

With self-awareness of your emotions, over time you can become more skilled at working through them.

Motivations Influence Your Crisis Response

We can better understand the natural tendencies in how humans respond to adversity through psychological motivation theories such as Maslow's Hierarchy of Needs. Abraham Maslow proposed that we have different human needs that must be met.

- Physiological — the need for air, food, water, sleep, health
- Safety — the need for safety, shelter, stability
- Belongingness — the need for love, belonging, inclusion
- Esteem — the need for self-esteem, recognition, respect, prestige
- Self-actualization — the need for development, creativity, growth.

The foundational, more primitive needs, physiological and safety, must be met before the basic needs of belongingness and esteem, and then the growth need of self-actualization, can be met.

When your primitive physiological and safety needs are threatened, your brain kicks into survival mode trying to meet those needs. A crisis threatens your needs at this very foundational level. Your natural tendency in a crisis, then, is to react with your primitive amygdala brain to quickly protect yourself from impending danger.

An ability to harness resilience during adversity produces a more thoughtful response and capacity to overcome these threats to your survival and growth potential.

> Timothy, a plant manager for a technology products manufacturer, was out on the production floor when he heard his name over the intercom: "Timothy, Line 1." He anticipated that this would be a routine call from his boss, Kayla, Vice President of Operations, needing a question answered or some information for a meeting. As he answered the line, "Hello, this is Timothy," he could already sense the anxiousness on the other end of the phone. "Our main component supplier's plant is on fire. We were expecting a large shipment tomorrow to run the order for our biggest customer. It will take at least six weeks for our backup supplier to ramp up and build enough extra parts to fulfill this order, causing our other customer orders to get backed up. This is a serious disaster. I need you in my office now to help figure this out." Tim sighed and scurried out of the plant. He knew it was going to be a long few weeks ahead.
>
> Worried, Tim could feel his breathing speed up a bit as he made his way to Kayla's office. Thoughts raced through his head... *What if we lose our biggest customer? We'll have to cut jobs. My job might even be cut. How will I pay the mortgage and feed my family? I've worked with so many of the people on this team for years. I'd hate to see anything happen to their jobs. I'll miss the camaraderie we've built around here. Production has been running so smoothly lately. How could this happen? Our team was even recognized recently for ten consecutive quarters of beating our operating plan. I was on track to be promoted next year. I told Kayla we needed a second back-up supplier. If she had just listened to me! Once our team hears about this, there will be more questions than I have answers to. What kind of answers can I come up with this time?*

As a leader, you're expected to have it all together, to be calm, cool, and collected... to be resilient. That's easier said than done, as you can see in Tim's case. He's walking into a tense situation. His guard is up. Naturally he's concerned, not just about the serious supply chain issue, but also about the broader impact this problem may cause.

How would you react in this situation?

Why Resilience Is Important in a Crisis

Resilience in leaders requires strong will, competent action, humility, and humanity. Once a crisis is at your doorstep, you have neither the time nor mental state to prepare to be resilient. You've got to be ready. Resilience Ready Leaders know that you will often face daily unexpected challenges that must be immediately addressed, and they are equipped to deal with them in a resilient manner. Resilience becomes second nature, an intuitive response to adversity.

"Resilience is that ability or set of capacities for positive adaptation, allowing you to keep in balance," states Linda C. Mays M.D. of the Yale Child Study Center.

"We're talking about the kinds of capacities, skills, and abilities that give people a sense of mastery and management of difficulty," adds Jack P. Shonkoff, Ph.D., of the Center on the Developing Child at Harvard University, in its video *What is Resilience?*

You're not born resilient. Resilience builds over time and begins development from experiences at the earliest stages of life. Situations children are exposed to in life, their environment, and the type of adult support they have when going through adversity, influence their ability to cope as they grow into adulthood. From these developmental experiences, some adults may have a greater capacity than others to effectively manage crises.

Resilience matures as you are tested and challenged, and as you grow from engaging resilience principles and behaviors that will cultivate your capacity, skill, and ability. #ResilienceReady

Keep in mind that resilience is a developmental process that continues through adulthood as you encounter various adverse situations. Resilience matures as you are tested and challenged, and as you grow from engaging resilience principles and behaviors that will cultivate your capacity, skill, and ability. Facing great challenges or traumas triggers higher levels of resilience. Your resilience level response capacity will influence your experience through the crisis as well as its outcome.

Resilience can be compared to the elasticity of a rubber band, with the ability to stretch under tension, yet return to its shape as pressure is relieved. A rubber band can be stretched multiple times in multiple ways and still maintain its utility. But if a rubber band is stretched beyond its capacity, it will break. The elasticity of a rubber band is built into its functionality. It's what a rubber band is. It is designed to retain its form.

Your resilience level response capacity will influence your experience through the crisis as well as its outcome. #ResilienceReady

The ability to bounce back, to be resilient, is within our human nature. But our resilience must be nurtured in order for us to call upon it when necessary.

Resilience is a critical crisis leadership skill. However, leaders and the organizations they lead are falling short. This is cause for *great* concern.

Remember:

- → Futurists predict that the crises we experience will be more frequent and pervasive.
- → Your ability to face ongoing industry- and business-level operational crises, rather than large-scale global crises, potentially poses the greater risk.
- → How you lead through times of crisis will dictate not only the health of your operations, but, more importantly, the health and commitment of your employees, customers, and business partners.
- → The leadership crisis that demands immediate attention: *Leaders are not prepared for the unrelenting crises that are more prevalent and emerging more rapidly.*
- → Emotions run high during a crisis. Be aware of a possible amygdala hijack. Before you act, process the emotion and what it is driving you to do.
- → Resilience in leaders requires strong will, competent action, humility, and humanity. You can't wait until a crisis hits to get prepared.
- → A developmental process, resilience matures as you are tested and challenged, and as you grow from engaging resilience principles and behaviors that will cultivate your capacity, ability, and skill.
- → Resilience is a critical crisis leadership skill. Leaders and the organizations they lead are falling short. This poses great cause for concern.

Chapter 2

The Consequences Are Costly

I would argue that the majority of companies don't have the resilience it takes to come out of a crisis strong. Companies are not preparing their leadership pipeline to lead with resilience. Leaders are not preparing themselves to be resilient. You hardly hear about resilience when referring to leadership and talent development initiatives. You rarely hear the word until a crisis hits. Then the need to be resilient becomes a common refrain. However, there's usually limited substance behind the actual practice of resilience. Simply marking time as the days go by, living through the crisis has little bearing on how resilient you really are.

A crisis by its very nature takes a toll on everyone affected. Fear and anxiety are commonplace, bringing myriad issues.

Going through a crisis with a lack of leadership resilience magnifies the toll on individuals and organizations as a whole, impacting both hard and soft business costs. When leaders are inept at resilience skills, the workplace creates additional pressure for you and your employees; stress levels escalate and work quality declines.

Going through a crisis with a lack of leadership resilience magnifies the toll on individuals and organizations as a whole. #ResilienceReady

It is important to face challenges and crises with a genuine concern for the safety and well-being of your team, your customers, and the communities you serve. This calls first for support of your employees at an individual level, in order to ensure they have what they need to be well, both personally and professionally.

> *"Nobody cares how much you know until they know how much you care."* — Theodore Roosevelt

A Closer Look at the Costs

Let's look at the implications, both at an individual leadership level and organizational level, of a lack of resilience.

Well-being: The Cost to Individuals

Meet Stephanie, a committed high achiever, one of the *A players* in your organization. She and her team always deliver. They call her the Energizer Bunny. She's at work early, stays late when needed, and is constantly connected to her work, even when she's not there. Due to a recent reorganization, Stephanie willingly took on additional responsibility, which also added staff to her team.

Outside of work, Stephanie serves as her daughter's Girl Scout troop leader, drives the carpool one day a week for her son's soccer team, performs with a musical ensemble, and serves on two community boards. Her goal is to get to the gym three days a week when she's not on the road. She and her husband are saving money toward the purchase of their next home, trying to avoid borrowing from their retirement savings.

Day in, day out; week in, week out… Stephanie works hard and gets it done. She has to find the power somewhere deep inside herself to successfully manage all these constant demands. She often wishes she had better support and resources at work and at home to help her consistently pull it all together. Though she doesn't realize it, Stephanie is trying to manage her overall well-being, which will impact all areas of her life.

You know some "Stephanies." You certainly have them in your own organization. You may even be one.

Stephanie is not alone. Deloitte found, in their Global Human Capital Trends study, *Leading the Social Enterprise: Reinvent with a Human Focus,* that with the accelerated pace of business and 24/7 constantly-connected working styles, more than 40% of all workers face high stress in their jobs. Work and life are no longer separate. Workers are always on. When going through a crisis, the demands on your workforce escalate. The result is a negative impact on productivity, health, and family stability… an impact on a person's overall well-being, as well as that of your organization.

If your organization is not more holistically focused on the state of an employee, beyond what typical wellness programs offer, you're failing to recognize a hidden impact on your business.

A more holistic view of well-being would include areas such as emotional, physical, financial, social/belonging, spiritual, and career/personal fulfillment. During my workshops and client coaching sessions, professionals share that crises take a personal toll, causing them to feel like they're on an emotional rollercoaster. Emotions and stress often show up in the following ways:

- Emotional well-being — panic, persistent worry, fear, doubt, confusion, anxiety, nervousness, anger, indecisiveness, sadness, loss, agitation, paralysis, insecurity, disappointment, lack of curiosity, pressure, frustration, depression
- Physical well-being — burnout, fatigue, exhaustion, lack of sleep, unhealthy eating habits, headaches, weight gain, high blood pressure, anxiety attacks, low energy, and other health problems
- Financial well-being — reduced income, debt, food insecurity, lack of savings
- Personal fulfillment — lack of confidence, low self-esteem, not living your dreams, not living up to your full potential, stagnation, feeling "less than," fear of making costly mistakes
- Social/belonging well-being — isolation, strained relationships, lack of trust, lack of communication, loss of community
- Spiritual well-being — unworthiness, diminished faith, disconnectedness, fear, pessimism, discouragement.

A crisis at work often brings about personal crises as well. When the well-being of your workforce is compromised, your capacity for a resilient, productive, and engaged workplace is at risk. In Gallup's Report, *Business Suffers When Your Employees Do*, results from their panel surveys show that "people with poor well-being...are less productive, less effective, less innovative and less perceptive. They cost more to insure, they're absent more often, less likely to be engaged, and have more safety and theft incidents." Therefore, organizations must rethink their wellness strategies to more holistically encompass well-being.

If your organization is not more holistically focused on the state of an employee, beyond what typical wellness programs offer, you're failing to recognize a hidden impact on your business. #ResilienceReady

Kentucky Performing Arts (KPA) recognized the need for a more holistic employee wellness strategy. Their Wellness in Action Initiative committed to meet the needs of the entire person, encompassing the areas of emotional resilience, social connections, financial well-being, and physical health. The programming and outreach efforts within the organization and surrounding community were guided by these overall goals: providing tools for growth, the compassion to act, and a sense of belonging.

When the well-being of your workforce is compromised, your capacity for a resilient, productive, and engaged workplace is at risk. #ResilienceReady

> "Our staff was seemingly living through one crisis after another, from a roof fire that halted business, to the significant restoration process that lasted a year and a half, all occurring simultaneously with an organizational restructure and the groundbreaking and subsequent opening of a new $12 million dollar venue. The impact these overlapping stressful events were having on the staff was palpable. We knew that the wellness initiative needed to provide an undergirding of support to allow them to heal, while also enabling them to remain agile as our organization evolved."
>
> Vicky Stevens, Director of Talent and Organizational Development, and founder/leader of the KPA Wellness in Action Initiative

As an example of programming that promotes emotional resilience, social connections, and physical health, and taking a cue from the creativity of the arts industry, Wellness in Action partnered with their programming team to avail artist groups to their full-time and part-time staff, as well as their volunteers. For example, prior to the onstage shows, members of DIAVOLO | Architecture in Motion treated staff and volunteers to expert-guided movement techniques and trust-building activities. Additionally, members of the Second City, Chicago's acclaimed improvisation theater company, led staff and volunteers through improvisational exercises as a way to connect through comedy, and to use laughter as a form of healing.

For its commitment to employee health and exceptional corporate health programming, Kentucky Performing Arts was named winner of the Healthiest Employers of Louisville award that year, a nationally recognized awards program powered by the Springbuk Health Intelligence Platform.

Consider This

Does your organization offer a wellness program or related services through your employee assistance program (EAP) that more holistically supports employees' overall well-being? Which of the following areas of well-being are addressed: emotional, physical, financial, social/belonging, spiritual and career/personal fulfillment, other?

Increased Business Risk

Workplaces are highly stressful, even in the absence of a crisis.

A global Korn Ferry study of 1,400 professionals worldwide found that "nearly nine in 10 professionals say work stress is getting worse." More than half of professionals surveyed felt that work-related stress was *much* higher than it was five years ago. Among the biggest contributing factors to heightened stress levels were heavy workload, a bad boss, organizational change, and the threat of job loss. A crisis can intensify all of these factors.

Deloitte's Human Capital Trends Study also shows that "People are working more hours, and problems of financial and mental stress seem to be at a peak."

Add a crisis to the stress levels already experienced in the workplace; the levels of strain and tension are intensified. During a crisis, the work environment is at a higher pace and more is expected of employees. Stress escalates.

Professionals shared with me that the levels of nervousness and pressure their bosses experienced during the COVID-19 crisis created a more toxic work environment. The brunt of that stress often gets directed at employees, whether consciously or subconsciously. One of my coaching clients shared that her team experienced elevated levels of stress from the lack of defined processes as they were going through change. As these preventable levels of stress continue, some of your best talent will shut down and do no more than what is required to get by. Others will voluntarily leave, even in a distressed economic climate.

The risk to your organization of ill-prepared leadership can be significant. In the *Future of Work: The People Imperative*, Deloitte reports that workplace stress costs global industry upwards of $300 billion per year in employee wellness, healthcare, and absence. Beyond the risk to operating results — greater revenue loss leading to deeper cuts in budgets, multiple rounds of layoffs, and a lack of investment back into the business — the more pressing risk is your human capital.

Using a stress assessment instrument is an ideal starting point to healing, helping individuals gauge their stress levels and contributors. As a leader, you can check in with individuals, and the team can explore ways to reduce or eliminate contributing factors.

An Opportunity for Change

Resilient organizations have vastly different experiences and outcomes. They prioritize equipping their leaders to effectively drive financial growth, as well as effectively bring their teams through a crisis. They go beyond creating risk management operating plans, ensuring an elevated focus on human connections. The human elements of their organizational culture and experience are treated as strategic priorities.

As a part-time faculty member at the University of Louisville College of Business, I experienced this first-hand through the COVID-19 pandemic and protests against racial injustice. One of the first moves Dean Todd Mooradian made as the pandemic hit was to check in on individual members of his team. He also quickly scheduled a virtual call for everyone to come together to share their concerns and support one another. He ensured that faculty and staff had the resources they needed to shift to online learning, and to personally deal with the crisis and stress as needed. The frequency and depth of these connections created a stronger sense of community and, I believe, healthier individuals and a team committed to the extra effort to get through those times.

Resilient organizations prioritize equipping their leaders for effectively leading financial growth as well as effectively leading their teams through a crisis. #ResilienceReady

A genuine concern for and investment in the well-being of your team members results in an overall healthier organization. The benefits far outweigh the costs. Employees are more committed, more engaged, and less stressed. These outcomes directly correlate to the bottom line in higher presenteeism (physically, emotionally, and psychologically), lower health care costs, lower turnover, greater teamwork and collaboration, greater innovation, and stronger operating results that lead to growth.

Which side of the cost equation you're on is up to you. Invest now or pay later. What will you choose?

Consider This

If you were listing employees on a balance sheet, would you list them as assets or liabilities? Why?

Remember:

→ Going through a crisis with a lack of leadership resilience magnifies the toll on individuals and organizations as a whole, impacting hard and soft business costs.

→ If your organization is not more holistically focused on the state of an employee, beyond that which typical wellness programs offer, there's a hidden impact on your business that you're failing to measure or address.

→ The risk to your organization of ill-prepared leadership can be significant, causing increased levels of employee stress and declining well-being.

→ Beyond the risk to operating results — greater revenue loss leading to deeper cuts in budgets, multiple rounds of layoffs, and a lack of investment back into the business — the more pressing risk is your human capital.

→ Using a stress assessment instrument to help individuals gauge their stress levels and contributors is an ideal starting point to healing.

→ Resilient organizations have vastly different experiences and outcomes. They prioritize equipping their leaders to effectively drive financial growth as well as effectively bring their teams through a crisis.

Chapter 3

Why Are Leaders Failing at Resilience?

No Rules of the Road for a Crisis

Have you ever watched a traffic intersection with stop signs? While writing this book, I sat facing a wall of windows looking out at a street with a four-way stop sign. It was interesting to watch how cars came and went through this intersection. Some drivers would come to a complete stop and then proceed through the intersection in the order they arrived. Some would kindly let everyone else go, including pedestrians, before proceeding. Others took driver privilege and did not yield for oncoming cars or pedestrians at all. When no other traffic was approaching, a few cars would roll through the stop sign, barely slowing down; occasionally, drivers were unsure and indecisive, not knowing whether they were going straight or turning right.

Then there were the pedestrians, either strolling or in a hurry, walking dogs or riding bikes. Most were fairly cautious when crossing the street.

When you approach an intersection, either driving or walking, you're supposed to know how to proceed. You're trained and preconditioned to understand how an intersection works... come to a complete stop; who goes first at a four-way stop; yield for pedestrians; watch for traffic in all directions before crossing the street. You do it all the time. The process has become intuitive, yet it still requires your attention and thoughtful consideration.

A skill for which we aren't trained nor conditioned is how to navigate the intersections of a crisis. #ResilienceReady

A skill for which we aren't trained nor conditioned is how to navigate the intersections of a crisis. We're not on automatic when crises occur. Each crisis is different and doesn't necessarily follow a structured set of rules. Crises can be as chaotic as the intersection I described. We can't approach them casually or callously. The process of dealing with crises requires high levels of attention and thoughtful consideration.

Emotions Add Complexity

Facing the intersection of a crisis is quite emotional. Sometimes you respond purely from that emotion, rather than reason, which can create one of two outcomes:

You let your gut or intuition drive decisions around the path you take, much like you do when you're driving a vehicle (that's how you get lost). You go by what feels natural or comfortable. You lean on the experience in making decisions, which can be helpful, but a crisis takes you into unchartered territory. Proceed with caution.

Facing the intersection of a crisis is quite emotional. #ResilienceReady

Or, you do nothing. You get stuck in the indecision of whether to turn or proceed forward. You're paralyzed by fear, letting others go ahead and around you until it feels completely safe.

The fact is, the path will never be completely safe or certain. You have to take calculated steps to move forward, making adjustments as you go.

When teaching them to drive, John Hackett, former president of Kroger's Louisville Division, told his children, "Just because the light is green, don't assume the path is clear. Look both ways before proceeding." That's a good rule of thumb.

Why Resilient Leadership Is Lacking

Growing up, you weren't taught how to get through a crisis with resilience, and it's typically not taught in leadership development either. The stress of a crisis can easily escalate, leaving you challenged with how to navigate through it, while keeping yourself, your team, and your organization intact (and maybe even in a better position when it passes). Resilience can seem impossible when you're in the middle of the struggle. If you don't develop resilience now and experience the practice of resilience principles, you won't know how to tap into your inner resilience when you need it most.

Let's consider three significant obstacles threatening your ability to operate with resilience and incorporate that resilience into your leadership practice:

- The walls of fear in your way
- The internal crisis you're fighting against fear
- Critical gaps in developing Resilience Ready Leaders

The Walls of Fear: Your Barrier to Progress

When you are in a place of fear, that's how you will lead. You want to come across as tough, so you don't admit your level of concern. Though you can learn to fight through them, your personal fears manifest in your leadership style. Fears impact your self-confidence, your courage, and your stamina to push through. If you suppress your fears and their accompanying emotions, rather than leading with authenticity, you end up creating the facade that everything is OK.

You also fail to realize what your team members are going through. They have similar experiences with fear.

Fear – The Science Behind Your Reaction

As human beings, we can sense a threat, and our natural instincts are to react from our emotions. I know when I'm walking and there's an unleashed dog ahead, my antennae go up because I've been chased by a dog before. I'm uncertain about what this dog is going to do, and if it's a certain breed of dog, I have a preconceived idea of what it is capable of doing.

We live with constant uncertainty. Nobody knows what will happen tomorrow. But as a leader in a crisis, the consequences of getting it wrong exacerbate fear and the internal instinct/response mechanism.

In his book *Thinking Fast and Slow*, Daniel Kahneman introduces the two systems of thinking that drive human response to stimuli. When System 1 Reactive Thinking kicks in, you respond based on the amygdala, the area of the brain that triggers the impulsive, emotional response. Environmental stimuli received through the senses — what you see, hear, touch, taste, smell — enter the amygdala first. Rather than thoughtfully processing what is coming into your brain from that stimuli, you make a quick reactive decision about what you believe is happening and what you need to do or say. You act without carefully considering the potential consequences.

Often stimuli evoke emotional responses based on prior experiences, biases, or assumptions. The amygdala is the most primitive part of the brain. It was critical for survival for our ancestors, who needed this limbic brain function to respond quickly to physical threats. The amygdala still serves you well, as there are times when you do need to make a quick response... such as in an emergency situation. (Crises certainly feel like emergencies, and sometimes they are.) Allowing the amygdala to rule your decisions and thought process can lead to trouble. In non-emergency situations, an amygdala response is usually not optimal.

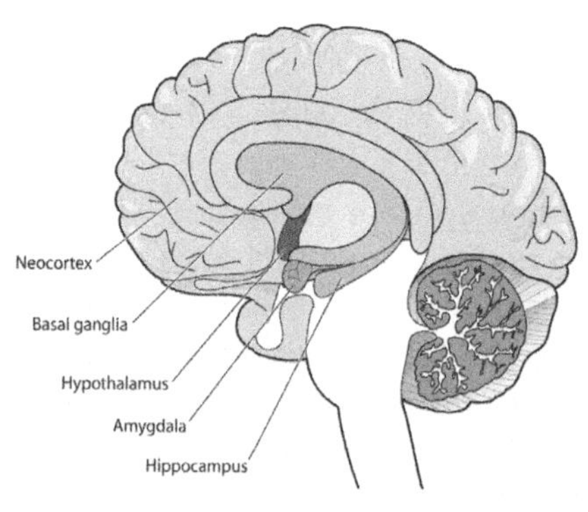

Here's how this may play out. You have completed a DISC behavioral styles assessment, which measures your patterns of behavior

— preferences, tendencies, and approaches to different situations across four dimensions:

- Dominance — problems, challenges, and exercise of power
- Influence — interactions with and influence of others
- Steadiness — change, variation, and pace of environment
- Compliance — rules, procedures, authority

Though overall behavioral patterns are most commonly a combination of two or more dimensions, one dimension is considered your primary behavioral style.

Let's say your primary behavioral style is High Dominance. Given the pressure from the urgency of a crisis situation, you're ready to make a decision and move forward. However, it may not be the best decision. Based on your System 1 Reactive Thinking you go by your gut, which tells you that you've seen a similar situation before. You may get frustrated when others need more time to process the situation, alternatives, and decisions. Your tendency is to move forward and make a decision on your own.

You get better results when you let the thoughts transition from your amygdala to the prefrontal area of the brain. According to Daniel Kahneman, this is where your System 2 Reflective Thinking kicks in. In this area of the brain, you can be more deliberate in processing the information coming into the brain from the stimuli to the amygdala to the prefrontal neocortex area. The outcomes of your decisions are more thoughtful and logical. Your emotions still play a role in this prefrontal deliberation, but how you use those emotions to your advantage is key.

Often when you're too close to an issue, you can't objectively move past where you're stuck. Rather than using Reflective System 2 thinking, you allow your emotions to feed your reaction.

The Three Walls of Fear

Three common fears are like towering walls that you can't traverse, inhibiting your ability to both operate with resilience and incorporate that resilience into your leadership practice. These walls are barriers to your progress.

Wall 1: Fear of Uncertainty

Wall 2: Fear of Loss

Wall 3: Fear of Failure

Do you see these in yourself?

Wall 1: Fear of Uncertainty

The uncertainty about what's ahead prevents you from dealing with the crisis. You realize things will no longer be the same, but you have no idea how they will turn out. You can't see that you can influence the future, positively or negatively, by the actions you take today. If only fear would step aside.

Sometimes you wish you were a kid again. Kids don't seem to fear anything. My neighbor told me about how her four year old granddaughter was ready to jump off the diving board at the pool. She had taken swimming lessons and was uninhibited by the challenge. As an adult, you have a responsibility to be mindful of what is ahead and consider the consequences of your decisions. But you can't let that uncertainty stop you from moving forward.

Sometimes you put up barriers and get in your own way. If you don't take the first step, the problem or change ahead of you will appear and remain bigger than it actually is.

Wall 2: Fear of Loss

When you're in a crisis facing change, especially when it seems the change was out of your control, you go through a series of emotions based on your perspective of the situation. It can feel like something was taken away from you, a decision was made that you didn't agree with, or you didn't have an opportunity to provide input.

I saw this vividly when my husband's former employer offered early retirement across the company in order to reduce labor costs. Some were excited and ready to retire. Others were not at a place in their lives emotionally or financially to retire, or felt like they would be left with nothing meaningful to do. They felt like they had so much more to contribute. They grieved the loss of what they knew and valued, and what gave them comfort.

Those who took a more hopeful perspective were able to deal with the transition with less anger and remorse. They could move on in a more thoughtful way to figure out what was next. My husband accepted the early retirement and worked through a process, making the decision to start his own business. Others took similar steps.

You have to go through some level of acceptance that there will be a new reality, and move into the Courage Stage of internal crisis response, which we'll discuss in the next section. Then you will be more in control of what happens to you as a result of this situation. Will you demonstrate resilience, or will you fall into victimhood?

Wall 3: Fear of Failure

Failure is typically viewed as a bad thing. Fear of failure puts you in a most vulnerable position. In her book, *Dare to Lead*, Brené Brown describes vulnerability as "the emotion that we experience during times of uncertainty, risk, and emotional exposure." As you think about this definition, what memories and emotions bubble up for you?

As if a crisis isn't risky and emotional enough, add to that a failure during a crisis and you think "I'm sure to be doomed." Some organizations do not tolerate risk or failure, even though they may say they do. Actions speak louder than words, so you would be hesitant to do anything for fear that if something went wrong, you'd put yourself in the vulnerable position of ridicule, and maybe even termination.

Lack of Confidence

Risk of failure can zap your confidence. You may have made decisions or taken action in the past that didn't work out, so now you're hesitant. You don't want to make the same mistake again. In mid- to high-stakes situations, you're more comfortable with either letting someone else make the decision for you or settling for what you've been doing… settling for what you know.

Imposter Syndrome

Imposter syndrome is the fear of being exposed. Lacking all the answers, your mistakes can trap you into trying to handle everything on your own. You try to create the appearance of having it all together, so you don't engage your team, the people who are most knowledgeable about your operations. This leaves your team feeling isolated, undervalued, and uninformed.

Consider failure differently — as a way of benefitting from your experiences, looking at the takeaways of what worked well, and learning from what didn't. Then try again.

When I ran customer experience for GE Consumer & Industrial, I was in a very high-visibility, politically sensitive role. I was responsible for working across each of the business units and product lines within our division to improve the customer experience and resulting Net Promoter Score metrics. I remember a particular meeting with a product general manager where I didn't have the answers to some of her research questions. Politically, I wasn't sure how to handle this situation for fear she would see me as an imposter. I made the wrong decision in agreeing that she would go directly to the research company to get the information, rather than personally taking the lead on the follow-up. In her mind, that diminished my reputation, which I then had to earn back. What I learned from that experience helped me to understand more about the needs of my internal clients and become a stronger strategic partner.

Failure is one of the greatest teachers and can strengthen your position as you move ahead.

Breaking Through the Walls of Fear

Getting through these three walls of fear can seem daunting. Your path around these walls begins with recognizing that fear is present, naming the types of fear you are experiencing, and identifying how those fears are manifesting internally, influencing your behavioral and emotional response. The Resilience Ready Principles and strategies introduced in Chapters 4 – 9 will be your pathway to managing these fears.

Consider This

Which Wall of Fear has inhibited your ability to be resilient in a recent crisis situation?

- Wall 1. Fear of Uncertainty
- Wall 2. Fear of Loss
- Wall 3. Fear of Failure

Fighting Your Internal Crisis

From Fear to Resilience: Five Stages of Internal Crisis Response

The second significant obstacle threatening your ability to operate with resilience and to incorporate that resilience into your leadership practice is your own internal crisis.

Going through a challenge can shut you down emotionally, often with serious physiological effects. While fighting the external crisis, you also have an internal crisis occurring. How you personally deal with a crisis affects how you lead others through a crisis.

©Vivian Blade

Five stages are characteristic of your internal response pattern when facing a crisis.

- Stage 1: Victim — You're in a state of denial. You blame others for what is happening and, therefore, others control your destiny. You're stuck in fear and despair.
- Stage 2: Settled — You've settled, though discontented, for the situation you're in because you feel powerless. You go along, business as usual, while the world changes around you.
- Stage 3: Surviving — You've made some changes in figuring out how to get by in the new normal. You're somewhat uncomfortable with the status quo, but fear, indecision, and lack of confidence keep you from taking steps to further improve your situation.
- Stage 4: Courageous — You have a strong desire for a better state of being. You take a calculated step forward, still vulnerable, but know things won't change unless you act.
- Stage 5: Thriving — You're taking consistent action toward a new future and can successfully operate in a new reality. The resilience principles guide you in working through the crisis and in making progress toward your goals. Taking action motivates you to keep going.

"Think of these stages as doors that you pass through as you move toward thriving," says Nackia Salmon, Aviation Services Cost Data Strategy Leader, GE Aviation. Some people never move beyond Stage 1 (Victim) or Stage 2 (Settled) where resilience is practically non-existent. If they do, a good number of people remain in Stage 3 (Surviving). You may go back and forth through the stages until you gain confidence and momentum from your progress. As you move through the stages, your resilience levels will grow.

Teams and organizations can also follow this response pattern, given the stages individuals of the team are in, their position of influence, and their willingness to adapt. Understanding the stages of internal crisis response and human tendencies will help you to be more empathetic to your employees' needs and how you can support them in building personal resilience.

As you build personal resilience, you're in a better position to inspire collective team and organizational resilience.

Let's explore each of these stages:

Stage 1: Victim

My initial response when I was laid off at GE was denial. I felt like a victim. I couldn't believe this was happening to me. I was fully committed to doing what was needed to help make our company successful... took on difficult assignments, worked late, missed dance rehearsals and little league games. Having been promoted to the executive level, I was moving up in the company and in my career. Why me? There was nothing I could do to reverse the decision. My career at GE ended.

> ***You know you're at the Victim stage when you refuse to accept your reality or any responsibility for changing it. #ResilienceReady***

You know you're at the Victim stage when you refuse to accept your reality. In the Victim stage you feel the greatest loss of control; rather, your circumstance controls you. You've ended up in a situation you say you didn't cause, didn't ask for, and weren't able to avoid. Perhaps you're in denial that this crisis could actually be happening to you and don't see a path forward. You feel like there's no way out.

During our interview, Tonya Jackson warned of teams getting stuck in the Victim Stage. "As you begin to face a crisis, there's a risk of the chaos and noise consuming you. People may talk about the crisis instead of focusing on understanding the crisis and developing actions to improve the situation. You may hear, 'How did this happen or who let this happen.' 'If we had invested in that project, this wouldn't have happened.' But it has 'happened' and here we are. And to move forward, you have to refocus your team on making decisions and taking actions to get out of the crisis."

Behavioral Characteristics

Victim behavior can show up as blaming others, not taking responsibility for your role in the situation, nor taking the steps to move out of it. You're angry at the people you feel are responsible for the situation. You may feel like others are purposely against you or don't care about you; the system did you wrong. Your anger shows up in strained relationships. You feel sorry for yourself, preferring to stay isolated and seeking pity from others (often subconsciously) as you sink into despair. You see yourself as not good enough. You don't deserve better. Your avoidance in making decisions allows others to call the shots, and you tend to go along.

You see the glass as completely empty. You lose hope. Your state of emotional, spiritual, physical, and social well-being in the Victim stage are often your lowest.

Consequences of This Stage

When you're in this mode, the sense of hopelessness often turns into negativity toward yourself and others. You function from a place of fear. Your level of vulnerability leaves you feeling exposed to such a degree that you turn inward, often isolating yourself from others. People don't want to be around you and often don't offer to help you, because you bring everyone else down. Your work quality suffers. You create a more stressful work environment for those around you.

Resilience in This Stage

Resilience is at its lowest point when you are in the Victim Stage. There is no space for resilience to form if you are not aware that you are in this stage nor open to accountability.

Stage 2: Settled

One of my coaching clients was dealing with a stressful work environment because of a toxic leader. This leader had been with the company for over twenty years, was politically connected, and was unwilling to receive constructive feedback. My client, worn down by the negativity and lack of support for her team, eventually gave up trying to address the concerns with her boss. She could get by everyday if she stayed out of her boss' path and made sure her team was staying on track. She began to settle for her situation until her health became noticeably affected. At that point, she knew it was finally time to reach out for help.

You know you're at the Settled Stage when you've begun to give in to your current situation. You don't really like the way things are but feel *this is just the way it is.* Efforts to get out of the situation didn't get you anywhere. You can't see an easy way out, and you've given up trying.

You know you're at the Settled Stage when you've begun to give in to your current situation because you feel powerless. #ResilienceReady

You begin to get comfortable with where you are. You settle in. You're coasting along and convince yourself that things are going OK. Why rock the boat? You can fly under the radar and no one really notices. You didn't cause this crisis, and you can't do anything about it. This too shall pass. You can ride it out.

Behavioral Characteristics

Your loss of a sense of meaningful purpose and opportunity causes you to lose interest and energy for the activities in which you once engaged. You can become isolated because you feel embarrassed when comparing yourself to your colleagues, friends, or family. Behavior can show up as sadness, transitioning into depression. You are being reactive, rather than proactive. You don't see a need to continue learning and growing, as it won't lead to anything. You feel like you don't have a voice, expecting that you have little influence over changing the situation. You "do what you have to do" at work to get by, believing that any extra effort will make little difference.

You see the glass as mostly empty.

Consequences of This Stage

When you're in the Settled Stage, your sense of helplessness often turns into complacency. You don't do much to help yourself when you are in this stage — you just go along for the ride. You don't speak up — you just meet the basic expectations of your job. People perceive you as less valuable. You exist in a position of fear. Relationships are strained as you may remain more isolated, and you fear sharing what is really going on inside of you.

Resilience in This Stage

Resilience continues to be at its lowest points during the Settled Stage. There is little space for resilience to form if you are not aware that you are in this stage nor open to accountability.

Stage 3: Surviving

Orlando knew that after the restructuring due to a merger, he was in a job that undervalued his skills and prior work experience. He wasn't fulfilled in his current job, but was making good money. He had a nice home, was able to take care of his family's needs, put away a little savings, and give to causes that were important to him. His life was busy in and out of work. He performed well in his role, but wasn't challenged or growing. There weren't many job opportunities to move into within his current company without going back to school for an advanced degree. Even then, a promotion would not be guaranteed. Alternatively, he'd have to look for a job at another company, but that came with even more uncertainty. Ultimately he decided to stay where he was and put a career change on the backburner.

You know you are in the Surviving Stage when you've figured out how to get by in the new normal. You've learned to "keep your head above water" and not draw any attention. You're uncomfortable with the status quo, but fear, indecision, and lack of confidence keep you from taking steps to improve your situation. Many people spend the majority of their careers in the Surviving Stage.

You know you are in the Surviving Stage when you've learned to "keep your head above water." #ResilienceReady

Behavioral Characteristics

You're in a game you know how to play. You know the ropes and it's going well. You're comfortable and making life work. There are times, though, when you get tired of being the victim or simply settling. You see that the world is moving on without you, and your lack of active engagement in your own destiny is resulting in unfavorable outcomes. You feel like you're ready to do more, to be more. You think about the possibility of change, that something different is possible, but it's not motivation enough to make a move, because fear and complacency are still in the way. The path to what could be seems overwhelming and unachievable.

You see the glass half full.

Consequences of This Stage

When you're in the Surviving Stage, you're running the same playbook day-in and day-out. You get busy with life as it is, in a routine that is not serving you as well as it may seem. You're not growing personally or advancing professionally. The circle of people around you are also surviving. You commiserate about your present state, and sometimes dream of other possibilities. Some days you may feel like *today is the day I'm going to make a change!* Other days, you lack the confidence to put yourself out there. The uncertainty with how things will turn out holds you back, causing you to miss out on opportunities. Others see you as not capable of much more than what you do now.

Resilience in This Stage

Resilience has some presence during the Surviving Stage. You've had setbacks to deal with, which you tend to sit in for a while. You find enough courage to keep going, but you're not rocking the boat. You're not moving forward, and, more often than not, disappointments and fear leave you frustrated and stuck.

Beware… many people don't move beyond this stage.

A Word of Caution

"As you are in any of these first three stages (Victim, Settled, and Surviving), your job might be vulnerable in the future in an organization undergoing lots of change. Like it or not, there is probably an unwritten list of employees who likely can't adjust to the new ways of doing business and you could be on that list," cautions former Kroger Division President, John Hackett.

If you remain in these three stages, you'll be viewed as ineffective and incapable of dealing with adversity, especially in a leadership role. Your business results and state of your team will prove this point. It won't be easy to move out of this stage, but the resilience principles shared in this book provide a roadmap to guide your way through.

Stage 4: Courageous

Your company's systems integration failure means you can't route customer service calls to the appropriate service agents. You've been patching the systems issues and surviving with service levels much lower than targeted. Though your teams are making it work, it's not the best you can do for your customers. The company has invested millions of dollars in the new system, but you know the right thing to do is to redeploy the old system and roll the new system back until the issues can be adequately addressed. This move will not only increase productivity, but, more importantly, reduce employee frustration and improve morale. Politically, this is a courageous recommendation to make, but your conscience won't rest until you can fulfill your promise.

You know you are in the Courageous Stage when your level of discomfort has gotten to a point where you're ready to do something about your current conditions. You're tired of just surviving and feel unsettled enough that your emotions wake up your complacency. Something happens and sets off a spark inside of you that says *maybe things don't have to be this way*. Nackia Salmon, Aviation Services Cost Data Strategy Leader for GE Aviation, describes this state of awareness as "when something hits a nerve and violates a promise you've made to yourself, or a core value, you just cannot be OK with the way things are anymore."

You know you are in the Courageous Stage when your level of discomfort has gotten to a point where you're ready to do something about your current conditions. #ResilienceReady

During the Courageous Stage, you've seen a sparkle of light. Hope reenters the picture. You begin to realize that you have more control over your situation than you thought. You're not quite sure what the answer is, but you've got enough motivation to try and figure it out.

Behavioral Characteristics

You begin to consider what it's going to take to change your current path. You imagine what *could be* in your future and what the first small steps should be. You're still apprehensive because you don't know how things are going to turn out, but you build up enough courage to give it a try. Nervous about taking a risk and the ambiguity of what's ahead, you feel vulnerable, so the danger is that you return to the Surviving or Settled Stage.

You see the glass as half full and rising.

Consequences of This Stage

The Courage Stage can be a springboard forward, if you don't allow the negative self-talk and naysayers to get into your head. If something doesn't go your way, it can seem like a setback. You begin to dig deep inside to find courage and stay focused on what is possible. It also can be easy to fall back into the Surviving Stage because moving forward seems so difficult and daunting. You take one step at a time.

Resilience in This Stage

Resilience has a greater presence because the resilience principles play a role in how you deal with the crisis. You have fewer setbacks, as you're being more proactive, and when setbacks do occur they don't have the effect of completely shutting you down.

Stage 5: Thriving

"We wanted to create a finance team in India and had started hiring people when COVID-19 became a reality and travel was put on hold," recalls Andrea Towns, a Fortune 500 finance executive. "So, we had to figure out how to grow a global team, with new people starting who knew nothing about our company, nothing about our systems, nothing about our finance structure; and have them be certified to be successful in this unique environment.

"It took really full dedication of changing the way we connect with people. Over several weeks we had daily calls with our India team just to make sure they were understanding how we work, introducing ourselves and the company, and acclimating them to our new environment. And it worked. They began just humming along. Some of my colleagues were very hesitant to grow globally in that environment for different reasons.

"But I've always thought of any challenge that comes your way, if you don't at least try it, then how do you know it won't work, and how can you say no? Now I can say we've been highly successful."

You know you are in the Thriving Stage when you are fully engaged in facing the crisis head on. You realize you have more control. You're much more proactive than reactive, influencing how things turn out, rather than being victim to the crisis. You've survived some bumps and don't give up easily on a tough challenge. Your courage and confidence have grown.

You know you are in the Thriving Stage when you are fully engaged in facing the crisis head on. #ResilienceReady

Behavioral Characteristics

During the Thriving Stage, you are on your path to getting through the crisis without it getting the best of you. You see the glass as full of opportunities and are hopeful that you can figure out a way to take advantage of them. You know you can't get through the crisis alone, and reach out to engage your family, friends, team, and needed experts for support and collaboration. You try to maintain a positive perspective and encourage others around you.

The Consequences of This Stage

You are beginning to make something happen. Owning your destiny gives you momentum and motivation to keep fighting. You realize that even when the road has not gone perfectly, you were actually OK. You have put aside some of the shame of imperfection, affording you the confidence to bring others in and work together. Many of your employees will see your confidence and become allies.

Resilience in This Stage

Resilience is at its greatest level during the Thriving Stage. The resilience principles are guiding you in your approach to addressing the crisis. The resilience principles activate as part of your normal operating mode, because you have developed resilience skills. You did not wait for the crisis to escalate before deciding that you needed to find some resilience in order to get through it.

Navigating Your Way to Thriving

Your journey through these stages is not necessarily linear. During a crisis, moving back and forth between stages is also likely. Given the nature of the crisis or the development of your resilience skill, your initial reaction is most likely to fall into either the Victim Stage, Settled Stage, or Surviving Stage. It will take intentional focus and recognition of your current internal crisis response to advance to the Courageous Stage or Thriving Stage. An important next step is moving your tendency to react in protection mode from your primitive amygdala brain into the region where you can more thoughtfully process your emotions, thoughts, and intention toward taking action.

Resilience will be critical to your capacity to get to the Thriving Stage. #ResilienceReady

Resilience will be critical to your capacity to get to and operate in the Thriving Stage. You will need to commit to developing your resilience skill before a crisis hits. The Resilience Ready Principles and strategies introduced in Chapters 4 – 9 will be your pathway to Thriving.

Consider This

Reflect back on a current or recent crisis. In which stage of Internal Crisis Response would you say you started? Where are you now? What was your journey like through the stages? Where did you find it difficult to move forward? Why?

Critical Gaps in Developing Resilience Ready Leaders

Leaders Are Not Prepared

Leaders are dangerously unprepared to guide their teams through a crisis. Critical gaps exist in the development of Resilience Ready Leaders, which is the third significant obstacle threatening your ability to operate with resilience, both personally and professionally.

It's not only individuals who get stuck at the intersection of fear and caution when navigating through a crisis; companies often operate in a similar fashion.

Companies are not developing talent in a manner that promotes leading with resilience, thus leaving leaders unprepared. #ResilienceReady

Most organizations have not equipped their leaders to prepare for or handle a crisis when it occurs, causing great consequence.

Three significant gaps companies must address:

- Gap 1: Lack of resilience training in leadership development
- Gap 2: Leadership development is not multidimensional
- Gap 3: Leadership pipelines are not diverse and inclusive

Gap 1: Lack of Resilience Training

Leadership development typically concentrates on the organizational values and leadership competencies that companies espouse will make them effective leaders. However, research shows that leadership development programs are not doing enough to prepare their participants to lead with resilience through a crisis.

PwC concludes from their Global Crisis Survey that "effective crisis management requires a combination of hard structure and 'soft' skills — the ability to handle the stress and chaos of crisis, to make decisions under pressure, to communicate the right messages in the right way to the right stakeholders."

Results of Deloitte's annual *Global Human Capital Trends study* consistently finds that companies are challenged with acquiring and developing future-ready leaders. Eight in 10 survey respondents said that "21st century leadership has unique and new requirements that are important or very important to their organization's success." Of those requirements, paramount was an "ability to lead through more complexity and ambiguity."

Though organizations are recognizing that the future environment will require resilience-related skills, they are not yet solving for it.

Gap 2: Leadership Development Is Not Multidimensional

In addition to the resilience-related skill sets and competencies missing in leadership development programs, companies are not taking a multidimensional approach to leadership development. While they may offer a series of leadership workshops, leadership competencies and resilience skills are developed over time using a multidimensional approach:

- Exposure to varied career experiences where leaders can develop critical skills
- Mentoring for feedback and guidance
- Sponsorship to ensure all talent is known and supported
- Career management to support professionals in achieving their career goals.

Many companies leave their rising talent to coordinate these additional important dimensions of development on their own. Talent development policies and practices are also outdated, lacking substantive focus on future needs due to the evolving business climate.

Gap 3: Leadership Pipelines Are Not Diverse and Inclusive

A lack of investment in preparing a diverse and inclusive pipeline of next-generation leaders has created a gap in available talent that is fully capable and ready when opportunities open up.

Minority groups are underrepresented in management occupations compared with the percentage of diverse populations in the workforce, according to statistics from Human Capital Media's Talent Tracker, which integrates data from open sources originating from the U.S. Census, the National Center for Educational Statistics, World Bank, and Bureau of Labor Statistics. McKinsey and Lean In report from their *Women in the Workplace* study that despite some progress, women are still underrepresented at every level of leadership. For women of color, the trends are even more concerning. They state that "without fundamental changes early in the pipeline, gains in women's representation will ultimately stall."

A lack of investment in preparing a diverse and inclusive pipeline of next-generation leaders has created a gap in available talent that is fully capable and ready when opportunities open up. #ResilienceReady

Most professionals responding to McKinsey's *Global Survey on Inclusion* report that "they encounter barriers to a sense of inclusion regardless of their gender, race, ethnicity, gender identity, or sexual orientation." The study also concludes that "respondents who feel very included in their organizations are nearly three times more likely than their peers to feel excited by and committed to their organizations."

Left unaddressed, companies lack the ability to be competitive in a dynamic marketplace, and risk higher turnover of their most promising diverse talent, higher cost to recruit, and a negative impact on employee engagement.

Closing the Gaps

These three gaps in developing Resilience Ready Leaders pose a significant threat to your capacity to attain a reliable and sustainable level of resilience required of your organization in the future. The Resilience Ready Principles and strategies introduced in Chapters 4 – 9 will provide a framework for the design of your leadership development program, practices, and training.

Consider This

To what degree are each of the Critical Gaps in Developing Resilience Ready Leaders a gap for your organization?

Use the following rating scale from 1 – 5 as described below:

1 Not a gap at all. We're doing great in this area!

2 Only a minimal gap. We have initiatives in place that address this area pretty well.

3 Somewhat of a gap. We have some initiatives that address this area, but need additional focus.

4 A vulnerable gap. We inconsistently give attention to this area. It could become a bigger problem in the future.

5 A serious gap. This area is not currently getting attention and needs to be addressed.

- Gap 1: Lack of resilience training in leadership development

  1 2 3 4 5

- Gap 2: Leadership development is not multi-dimensional

  1 2 3 4 5

- Gap 3: Leadership pipelines are not diverse and inclusive

  1 2 3 4 5

These Significant Obstacles Should Be Concerning

Lack of resilience among leaders is a serious concern. There are potentially significant consequences to you as an individual and to your organization from being ill-equipped to overcome fear with resilience.

The obstacles addressed in this chapter that are inhibiting the development of prepared, resilient leaders can be overwhelming. There are steps you can take starting now.

You first want to identify the obstacles threatening your organization's capacity for facing crises with resilience. Follow through by determining and committing to actions to eliminate these obstacles.

Chapter 4 will outline a framework introducing the resilience principles and how the skill development process works.

Chapters 5 – 9 provide a deep dive into each of the resilience principles that you will integrate into your leadership and organizational resilience capabilities.

Let's get started.

Additional resources are available at ResilienceReady.today.

Remember:

→ If you don't develop the skill to build resilience and don't experience the practice of resilience principles, you won't know how to reach your inner resilience when you need it most.

→ Three significant obstacles threaten your ability to operate with resilience and to incorporate that resilience into our leadership practice:

- The walls of fear in your way
    - Wall 1: Fear of Uncertainty
    - Wall 2: Fear of Loss
    - Wall 3: Fear of Failure
- The internal crisis you're fighting against fear

  Five Stages of Internal Crisis Response
    - Stage 1: Victim
    - Stage 2: Settled
    - Stage 3: Surviving
    - Stage 4: Courageous
    - Stage 5: Thriving
- Critical gaps in developing resilient leaders
    - Gap 1: Lack of resilience training in leadership development
    - Gap 2: Leadership development is not multidimensional
    - Gap 3: Leadership pipelines are not diverse and inclusive

→ These significant challenges should be concerning. There are potentially significant consequences to you as an individual and to your organization from being ill-equipped with resilience.

PART 2

THE RESILIENCE READY LEADER'S GUIDE

Chapter 4

Solving the Leadership Crisis: Becoming Resilience Ready

During a crisis, you can feel like you're on a high-speed bullet train taking you to a place you've never been before and don't want to go. You were pushed onto the train. This journey certainly was not by choice. Reality sets in. Now that you're on the train, you must contend with the hand you've been dealt. As you ride along, everything seems to pass by in a blur.

The Resilience Ready framework of leadership competencies and practices are essential for resilient leadership in the new reality of uncertainty and ambiguity. #ResilienceReady

While you may not have had control getting on the train, you do have some controls at your disposal while riding it. You can dictate what commands your attention while on this train. You navigate your way to the most appropriate stop, getting off where it leads you closest to your destination. Instead of riding aimlessly on the train, you can move into the conductor's seat, navigating and steering your train to the best outcome for your organization. You don't have to go wherever the train takes you. You can choose and navigate a new route, a new direction, a new destination, one that you would never have imagined or discovered had you not been in this crisis.

Aimlessly stuck, stressed, and disappointed does not have to be the train you ride through a crisis. New opportunities often emerge from a crisis if you open yourself to them. Crisis creates disruption. Position yourself to take advantage of those opportunities. You can only do that if you are Resilience Ready.

No More Playing It Safe

Fear and anxiety can cause you to become complacent, stuck in the Surviving Stage, or worse, stuck in the Victim Stage or Settled Stage, sitting on the sidelines and watching opportunities pass by. You feel stuck in a time warp that seems out of your control. You watch others who seem to have it all together as they speed past you with what seems like minimal effort and concern. They're moving on unscathed, or so it appears. You feel stuck, not knowing what to do, afraid you'll make the wrong move; so you do nothing. You wait for the right time to make a move, but it feels like there never is one. You don't have it all together. Nothing is perfect. You're afraid of making a mistake. Your organization doesn't take too kindly to people who take a risk and make a mistake. You'd rather play it safe and stay in the passenger seat; stay in your comfort zone. But on this journey, safety is an illusion.

When you step outside your "safe zone", more will be revealed, enabling you to observe the situation with greater clarity and objectivity. You'll open up to the community on the journey with you — family, friends, colleagues, customers, suppliers — giving you opportunities to spend time with them, talk with them, see how their world has changed. How have their needs shifted? What are their greatest fears? What opportunities do they see ahead? How have their needs from you changed, and how can you collaborate to meet those needs? How can you be a source of light and hope, to be a partner in finding solutions to help them get through this crisis?

Consider This

What fears tend to keep you inside your comfort zone? What inspires you to move outside your comfort zone?

Resilience Empowers

Adversity is certain. Resilience empowers you to work through adversity, enabling you to step outside your "safe zone" to face the pending unknown with greater confidence. You experience more personal growth moving through adversity than at any other times in your life.

According to the American Psychological Association, "psychologists define resilience as the process of adapting well in the face of adversity, trauma, tragedy, threats, or significant sources of stress."

People and organizations that exhibit resilience demonstrate an ability to manage, albeit not always perfectly, changing conditions during a crisis. Resilience begins with a mindset or perspective that it is possible to get through the crisis. You find the courage to step out of your safe zone to move forward.

According to the American Psychological Association, "psychologists define resilience as the process of adapting well in the face of adversity, trauma, tragedy, threats or significant sources of stress." #ResilienceReady

Tonya Jackson shared with me that "Resilience is believing there's a path forward, fully acknowledging that it might be bumpy, it might be rocky, it might be messy, but we can get through it. The outcome might not be perfect, but we're going to be in a better spot. Perfection is not the goal because there is rarely a perfect decision in a crisis. Most importantly, resilience is a conviction and belief that we can move forward."

Learning takes place through the process of moving forward, especially when things don't go your way. You have the wherewithal to get back up and try again when you're knocked down. Resilience returns a sense of hope and brings composure when you feel like chaos is occurring around you. Even when you have a crisis or disaster recovery plan, the road is going to be scary and uncertain. Resilience gives you the "how" blueprint, around which your crisis management plans can take shape and be executed.

Resilience gives you the "how" blueprint, around which your crisis management plans can take shape and be executed. #ResilienceReady

Being resilience ready does not mean that you won't face crises, or that you are supposed to emerge as the smartest, most strategic person who makes it through flawlessly. Your approach to navigating through a crisis, and the humanity you show as you lead others through it, demonstrates your resilience.

Consider This

Think of a recent challenge your team faced. To what degree was there concern related to the emotional or physiological impact on employees and customers?

Building and Flexing Your Resilience Muscle

The heart is central to the body's cardiovascular system. It is a muscle that you have to build up and take care of in order to get it in the best possible shape. Your heart pumps blood and oxygen to every part of your body. Like other functions of your autonomic nervous system, this is involuntary. You don't have to think about it. If your heart is healthy, it performs this function well.

Your approach to navigating through a crisis, and the humanity you show as you lead others through it, demonstrates your resilience. #ResilienceReady

---

To ensure your heart is healthy, you have to invest in cultivating a healthy heart. It requires you to eat well, exercise, avoid smoking, and forgo other habits that could damage your heart. You don't wait until you have heart trouble to try and build up your heart muscle. Once you've had a heart attack, the heart muscle is weaker, and it is much harder to build its strength back up. Building your heart muscle requires that you work on keeping it healthy when you are well, to build up the strength to prevent heart problems or minimize the degree of damage and illness that a heart issue could cause.

Resilience is like a muscle that is always there working on your behalf. You don't even have to think about it. When you're facing a challenge, if you don't have a reservoir of resilience to call upon, if you don't know where to find resilience deep inside of you, it's going to be tough to get through it. You'll find yourself stuck in the Victim Stage, Settled Stage, or Surviving Stage, responding from persistent fear and lack of control.

You build up resilience by building your skill in the resilience principles and applying those principles in how you live and lead each day. Consider how exercise works for your heart muscle and other muscles in your body. You select specific exercises to build specific body parts. Bicep curls and push-ups strengthen your arms and chest muscles. Running and aerobic exercise strengthen your cardiovascular system. You work out on a regular regimen and combine that with other practices, such as eating more fruits and vegetables, and drinking plenty of water. As you continue that practice you maintain strong muscular and cardiovascular systems, and, ultimately, a strong and healthy mind and body. You follow and practice the principles of health consistently each day.

There will be times when you get out of the routine, but the habits you've formed and the state of wellness you've grown accustomed to pull you back. For example, when my schedule gets extremely busy with travel and consulting with clients, finding time for exercise sometimes gets put on the back burner. Before long I will have less energy and become more fatigued. My body is admonishing me to get back to that consistent activity. As I return to my routine exercise schedule, I return to greater focus, productivity, and overall wellness.

Your Blueprint – The Resilience Ready Principles

Resilience comes from your reservoir of willpower and stamina to stay in the game. Like your physical wellness, resilience is not a static state of being or a destination to which you arrive and remain. Your resilience naturally fluctuates due to the circumstances of a crisis,

You have to work at recharging your resilience specifically to deal with the crisis at hand. #ResilienceReady

other challenges you are concurrently dealing with, and your stage of internal crisis response at a given point in time. You have to work at recharging your resilience specifically to deal with the crisis at hand. Every crisis you face will be a unique experience and will affect you differently.

Your resilience builds through practice — even when times are *not* tough — so that your habits formed around these principles are ingrained when tough times emerge and you need them. You become *Resilience Ready*.

The principles and practices I guide you through in this book offer a framework for rebuilding your reservoir of resilience so that you can adjust to, and purposefully deal with, challenges as presented through the crisis.

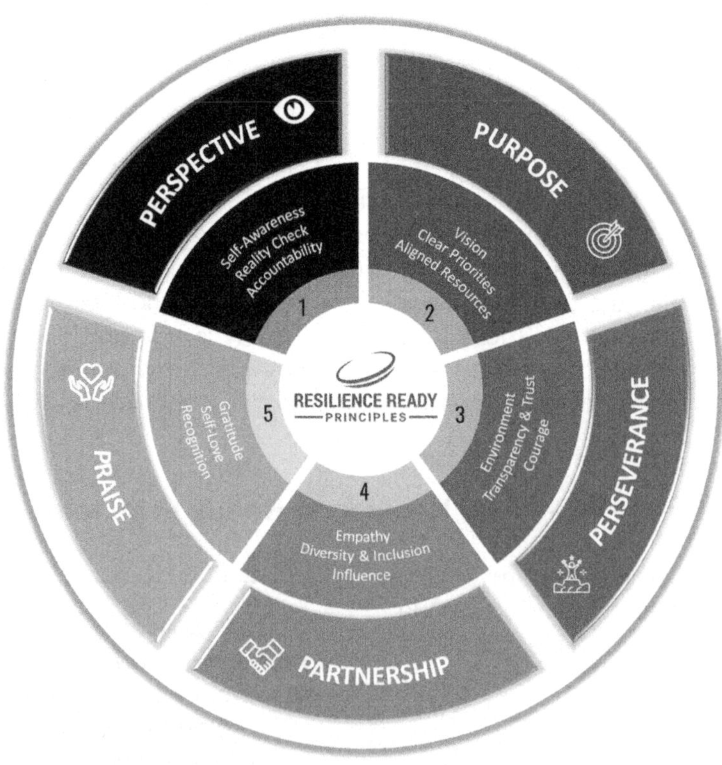

©Vivian Blade

The five Resilience Ready Principles to get you through a crisis are:

1. Perspective (Chapter 5)
2. Purpose (Chapter 6)
3. Perseverance (Chapter 7)
4. Partnership (Chapter 8)
5. Praise (Chapter 9)

These principles are essential in facing significant business and day-to-day challenges. We'll go deep into each principle in the upcoming chapters.

You have probably heard the saying "When the going gets tough, the tough get going." With these five resilience principles, you'll have the foundation to get tough *and* to get going!

The Role Servant Leaders Play in Building a Culture of Courageous Resilience

I encourage you to think about what your role as servant leader in a crisis really could be... are you a passenger on the high-speed train or are you the conductor? Fear can convince you to remain a passenger, simply dealing with challenges as they arise.

As a *leader*, your given role is to be the conductor, guiding your team in charting a new path. As a *servant leader*, your greatest opportunity is making a human connection with the community going through this with you. How do we get through this together and be a better, stronger team as we move beyond the crisis? You have the power to step up to this role.

In his book, *Servant Leadership in Action*, Ken Blanchard describes servant leadership as "an influence process in which you try to help people accomplish goals." He demonstrates that servant leadership is comprised of two parts:

- "A visionary/direction or strategic role — the **leadership** aspect of servant leadership; and
- An implementation, or operational, role — the **servant** aspect of servant leadership."

Blanchard further explains that "the **servant** aspect of servant leadership is all about turning the (traditional organizational) hierarchy upside down, and helping everyone throughout the organization develop great relationships, get great results, and, eventually, delight their customers. That's what servant leadership is all about."

Are you stepping up to this role?

As you forge ahead as conductor of that high-speed train, know that the twists and turns are going to be rocky for your passengers. Just as you have to work through the crisis emotionally, so does your team. Leading with resilience requires humility and humanity. Humility in being transparent to the fact that the crisis is also tough on you. Humanity in the compassion and empathy you have for your team as you support them in their individual and collective journeys to resilience.

Your role is to guide your team in building their resilience muscles. You want to build not just a temporary response to get you through the crisis, but a culture of resilience that permeates throughout your organization and becomes a competitive advantage.

Leading with resilience requires humility and humanity. #ResilienceReady

Organizations aren't resilient without the ability of their people to discover and thrive from their places of personal resilience.

Therefore, resilience skill is required at the individual and team levels. Resilience begins at an individual or personal level. We'll focus there first.

Inspiring Personal Resilience

You have what it takes to be successful. Sometimes you just have to tell fear to step aside. You have to tell the negative voices inside your head that they are not welcome. At times, those negative voices come from other people. Sometimes people mean well and don't realize the damper they are putting on your dreams. Let go of the white noise; in one ear and out the other. Never doubt your capabilities.

You can make the required mental shift and find the courage to move forward. What matters are the little decisions you make and the small steps you take toward making change happen.

Everyone approaches a crisis differently. Your personality, behavioral drives, and life experiences all contribute to how you see the world and work through change. You don't have to try to be somebody else. Integrate your personal approach with the steps that follow.

Your Awareness, Intention, and Commitment Required

The road to building your personal resilience muscle requires your awareness, intention, and commitment to the ongoing work. You'll also need to give yourself some grace for the imperfection you'll experience as you learn, practice, and adapt these principles to any given crisis you face.

The road to building your personal resilience muscle requires your awareness, intention, and commitment to the ongoing work. #ResilienceReady

---

The following steps will guide you in becoming Resilience Ready, free from being stuck in the Victim Stage to living and leading in the Thriving Stage:

- ***Grasp the principles*** — This book takes you in-depth on each of the five Resilience Ready Principles. Read, study, review, and understand the principles and associated leadership practices.

- ***Identify and address the obstacles to becoming Resilience Ready*** — You have to know where you currently stand in order to map out a path to change. Identify and prioritize the specific obstacles that need to be addressed to begin deepening your personal resilience skill. Complete the Resilience Ready Self-Assessment to identify where you currently stand in your resilience readiness and the contributing factors. Get feedback from your team and others who are familiar with your leadership by having them complete the Resilience Ready Feedback Survey.
- ***Take action toward becoming Resilience Ready*** — Everyone is different, and your experience and needs through a crisis will vary. Discover areas across the five Resilience Ready Principles that would help strengthen your resilience right now. Utilize the reflections, recommended actions, and resources that accompany this book to enhance your skill across the Resilience Ready Principles. Engage a mentor or executive coach to help you explore ideas and keep you accountable.
    - *Practice the Resilience Ready Principles* — Identify opportunities to integrate the Resilience Ready Principles into your life and leadership practice. Align your practice of these principles to your personality, values, leadership style, and needs. Be intentional about putting the principles and strategies into practice without expecting everything to go perfectly.
    - *Reflect and adjust* — Reflect on the outcomes of your practice. Was the result what you expected? What would you repeat or do differently next time? Retake the self-assessment to see how your resilience readiness has evolved. Commit to ongoing learning, development, and practice.

Inspiring Team Resilience

As you build your personal resilience skill, you will be able to support and encourage others in building theirs. Your goal as a servant leader is not to be the resilient hero who saves the organization from doom. It won't happen, no matter how much you dream it. Be a role model in demonstrating resilience, even when you don't necessarily feel confident. Engage your team in working through the disruption together.

You'll find that the Resilience Ready Principles inspire leadership practices that align with many servant leadership competencies. In the book, *Servant Leadership in Action*, author Larry C. Spears, former President & CEO of the Robert K. Greenleaf Center for Servant-Leadership, summarizes ten of the most important core characteristics and beliefs of servant leaders from the work of Robert K. Greenleaf, founder of the modern servant leadership movement:

- *Listening* — Listens intently and receptively to what is said and not said; and hearing one's own inner voice.
- *Empathy* — Strives to understand and empathize with others.
- *Healing* — The potential for healing one's self and one's relationships to others.
- *Awareness* — General awareness, self-awareness, an ability to view most situations from a more integrated, holistic position.
- *Persuasion* — Seeks to convince others, rather than coerce compliance.
- *Conceptualization* — Thinks beyond day-to-day realities to look at a problem or an organization from a conceptualizing perspective, nurturing their abilities to dream great dreams.
- *Foresight* — The ability to foresee the likely outcome of a situation based on lessons from the past, the realities of the present, and the likely consequence of a decision for the future.
- *Stewardship* — Holds a commitment to serving the needs of others with openness and persuasion rather than control.
- *Commitment to the growth of people* — Deeply committed to the growth of each individual within the organization, believing that people have an intrinsic value beyond their tangible contributions.
- *Building community* — Identifies some means of building community among those who work with and are connected to a given organization.

Resilience is integral to servant leadership. Its strength is in managing beyond the operational activities to empowering your team members with the capacity to thrive.

Provide training and support and build a culture that helps employees develop and practice their resilience skills. Integrate the *Inspiring Personal Resilience* steps outlined above with your team. The accompanying workbook includes discussion questions for each of the resilience principles that you can use with your team to inspire team resilience.

Resilience is integral to servant leadership. #ResilienceReady

The results will be growth into an extremely strong, road- and weather-tested individual, team, and organization that can stand the test of time.

Inspiring Organizational Resilience

To close the gap on building resilient leaders within your organization, design a leadership development training program based on the resilience principles that address your specific needs. These resilience principles can be aligned with the values and competencies important to your organization's success. Define associated behaviors that integrate the principles into the organizational culture.

There may be times when an organization's values (stated or not) are counter to resilient servant leadership and will need to be re-examined. For example, when budgets are tight during a crisis, one of the areas often cut is employee training and development. The lack of investment in employee upskilling or professional development not only communicates that they are less valued, but also creates gaps in your organization's talent capabilities. "You pay for training whether you budget for it or not," cautions John Hackett.

Leadership development on this resilience framework should become part of your succession planning strategy. Build a leadership bench and pipeline of talent who are capable and confident in capitalizing on the upside of the crisis and returning the company to growth and profitability. More importantly, they will be equipped and accountable ambassadors of the humanity, support, and community that employees, customers, and partners need in order to get through these times.

Your Roadmap Ahead

This book includes leadership competencies and practices that are non-negotiable for becoming a Resilience Ready Leader who is prepared to effectively lead both operations and human capital through uncertainty and ambiguity.

In the following chapters we'll unpack each of the Resilience Ready Principles. We'll explore why each principle is important in becoming a resilient individual and leader, and you'll have a guide at your fingertips of day-to-day practices to build your resilience skill.

It's time to lead with resilience!

Remember:

→ Adversity is certain. Resilience empowers you when working through adverse times, enabling you to step outside of your "safe zone" to face the unknown with greater confidence. You experience more personal growth moving through adversity than at any other times in your life.

→ Being resilient comes from your approach to how you get through a crisis and the humanity you show as you lead others through it.

→ You build up resilience by building your skill in resilience principles and applying those principles to how you live and lead each day.

→ The five Resilience Principles that are essential in getting you through a crisis are:

- Perspective (Chapter 5)
- Purpose (Chapter 6)
- Perseverance (Chapter 7)
- Partnership (Chapter 8)
- Praise (Chapter 9)

→ As a servant leader your role is to guide your team in building their resilience muscles. You want to build not just a temporary response to get you through the crisis, but a culture of resilience that permeates throughout your organization.

→ Resilience skill is required at the individual, team, and organization levels, but must begin at an individual level.

CHAPTER 5

Perspective

RESILIENCE READY PRINCIPLE 1

"What you're thinking is what you're becoming."
— Muhammad Ali

"Life is 10 percent what you make it and 90 percent how you take it." — Irving Berlin

"I admit it," says Tim, a plant manager for a technology products manufacturer. "When I first walked into my boss Kayla's office, the Vice President of Operations, I was pessimistic about how we were going to solve this supplier parts issue fast enough to minimize the long-term impact." As Tim entered the room, several other leaders were already gathered at the table — Veena, VP of Finance, Hakeem, VP of Sourcing, Cynthia, Product Manager, and Jacob, Sourcing Manager. "I could feel the tension. The conversation began with trying to figure out who was to blame that we were in this position. We were left hanging, not having enough backup suppliers ready to meet our component orders in a crisis situation. There were no quick solutions," he lamented.

"Once we got past the initial shock and defensive reactions, we realized we needed to adjust our approach to this problem. First, we each had to check in on ourselves — how were we feeling? What was triggering our emotions, and how was that causing us to respond to the crisis and to each other? Then, we began to lay out the facts to get a clear picture of what we were dealing with. Finally, we had to commit to do our part and pull in the resources that would be needed to solve this as quickly as possible.

"This shift helped us to change our perspective. It honestly took us a few days to get to this point. But we could see that if we and our teams could work better together, we could come up with a workable solution. And if we were positive, yet realistic and transparent, we could rally our teams to put positive energy behind this."

Why Perspective Is Important to Achieving Resilience

In the heat of adversity, it's hard to see beyond the immediacy of what's going on right in front of you. While trying to mitigate potential damage, it's easy to get caught up in the moment, in the drudgery of the work required to get through these times. You call yourself a realist. Just give you the facts and you'll deal with them. You don't want to be a Pollyanna and give false hope, and you certainly don't want to sugarcoat the situation.

The lens through which you view today's reality colors the lens through which you see and realize your future. #ResilienceReady

It's essential to face reality. However, reality should *inform* your future, not dictate it. The lens through which you view today's reality colors the lens through which you see and realize your future.

A leader's perspective influences others. Employees and customers will take cues from how you handle a situation. They can tell when you're stressed or uneasy. They can tell if you believe in what you are telling them. If you are anxious, employees and customers will be as well.

When you have a more hopeful perspective, you reclaim control of the situation. #ResilienceReady

Your objective in this stage is to make a mental shift about the situation and possibilities. Your team and organization need you to show up as a leader with a "can-do" positive outlook. Even though tough decisions must be made during a crisis, your perspective on how those decisions generate positive outcomes for the organization is essential.

When you have a more hopeful perspective, you reclaim control of the situation. You refuse to settle or become a victim, but rather you're empowered to create a better future.

Consider This

In my role as chair of the Board of Directors of Girl Scouts of Kentuckiana, I was extremely proud of the impact a single girl could make in the lives of others. Gold Award Girl Scouts, those who have achieved the Girl Scouts' highest honor, are leading the way to solve some of the world's greatest societal crises. These high school-aged Girl Scouts select a problem in the world or their community about which they are passionate.

To earn the award, they must work with the associated organizations and constituents to complete a seven-step process that leads to the implementation of meaningful solutions to bring about lasting change. Gold Award Girl Scouts are addressing issues such as human trafficking, the gender gap in STEM, literacy, and food insecurity... major societal problems. Their attitude *could be* that these issues are much bigger than one girl could possibly solve. Their perspective *is* that they have power to make the world a better place. And they *are*... one girl at a time!

For more information on Gold Award Girl Scouts, visit https://www.girlscouts.org/en/our-program/highest-awards/gold-award.html

---

How a Crisis Impacts Perspective

Beware

Your outlook is heavily shaped by your surrounding environment. During a crisis there is a lot of fear and anxiety created from the constant news and chatter. Much of what you hear is sensationalized negativity. Even when you find yourself trying to stay informed, the overflow of information tends to direct your outlook toward itself. That instigates an emotional response which may not necessarily be a rational outlook on the situation. Especially early on, the news and chatter are doom and gloom, much of which comes from the fact that there is little information and many unknowns.

Your environment includes people around you who have different ideas and perspectives. It's good to get diverse opinions and input. Welcome it. Keep in mind that people you trust and care about heavily influence your own thinking and outlook. You also see what other people are experiencing and fear that the same will happen to you.

In an attempt to process all of the information flooding in, your brain instinctively goes into its primitive survival mode by activating the brain's amygdala. You react quickly to protect yourself, whether or not that response is best for you. You respond to the situation along either side of the spectrum. On one side you see it as hopeless, too difficult to deal with. You are pessimistic about possible outcomes and believe you lack control to change the inevitable. On the other side, you see the situation as difficult, but are hopeful about a manageable outcome. Your thoughts about the situation move from your brain's amygdala to your prefrontal cortex, giving you the opportunity to more thoroughly contemplate the situation and explore the possible outcomes with greater objectivity.

Your biases and preconceived notions enter your judgments and perceptions without you even thinking about it.

Andrea Towns, a Fortune 500 Finance Executive, encourages leaders to have self-patience: "People have to be patient with themselves. There's a lot going on in everybody's life. It's okay to be scared, afraid, and to not know what to do, whether it's related to your job or related to something at home. Life can be tough sometimes. So, be patient and surround yourself with people who will allow you to be, and who will protect your thoughts as if they were their own."

Consequences of a Pessimistic Perspective

"The optimist sees the donut; the pessimist sees the hole."
— Oscar Wilde

In a crisis, if you permit an amygdala brain response to take over, an emotional hijack, you'll tend to react quickly in order to protect what you believe is in imminent danger. Whether conscious or not, your biases come into play. You form an instant opinion about what is going on and why. This System 1 thinking, the thought process described by psychologist Daniel Khaneman, is not based on objective facts, but on preconceived perceptions, past experiences, societal stereotypes, and hearsay. This response may not be the best or most thoughtful.

A pessimistic view of the situation and its possible outcomes brings on worry and stress, which impacts your personal and organizational well-being. I bet you can recall times when worry and despair about work or a personal concern weighed heavy on your heart and mind. You may experience a loss of appetite or find it difficult to sleep. You can't stop thinking about what worries you.

A pessimistic view of the situation and possible outcomes brings on worry and stress, which impacts your personal and organizational well-being. #ResilienceReady

Pessimism steals your sense of empowerment and control. You feel like the situation dominates. This causes you and your organization to get stuck in the Victim Stage of internal crisis response. It's like being stuck in quicksand. You don't know what to do and you're afraid to act. You're going under and there's nothing you can do about it. This lack of action only exacerbates your dilemma.

You've likely heard the familiar sayings "one bad apple spoils the whole bunch" and "a negative attitude spreads like wildfire." Negativity is like a virus moving from one person to another. As a result, your work environment will be permeated with low morale, low employee commitment, and disengagement. These conditions turn into low productivity and higher rates of employee absenteeism and turnover.

The negative environment will bleed into customer relationships and the customer experience. It's easy for customers to tell when employee morale is low. It comes across in peer and customer interactions. Your products and services will not meet the evolving needs of customers during a time when they most need you.

Advantages of a Positive Perspective

On the contrary, a positive, hopeful perspective has a profound impact on the potential at an individual and organizational level. A "glass full of opportunities" outlook reduces worry and stress and improves overall well-being, including better sleep, disposition, eating habits, and general health.

Positive perspective manifests in hope, which brings energy for taking action and moving ahead through a course that still is likely to be arduous. You can remove the victim mentality and move on to being courageous and accountable for doing what it takes to prevail.

With a positive perspective, you can remove the victim mentality and move on to being courageous and accountable for doing what it takes to prevail. #ResilienceReady

When you have a positive mental attitude, you feel better about yourself. Positivity can spread as well. When people feel better about themselves, they can manage fear and anxiety, and believe that there are better days ahead, thus creating a more positive and motivating work environment. As a result, your employees will experience better morale. Increased employee commitment and engagement will generate higher productivity, lower rates of employee absenteeism, and less turnover.

Steps to Becoming Resilience Ready

Steps to Shift Your Perspective

What can you do to shift your perspective? There are three steps in your toolkit:

Step 1. Enhance your ***self-awareness***
Step 2. Take a ***reality check***
Step 3. Power-up your ***accountability***

These steps include both an inward- and outward-facing perspective. Ask yourself… What do I know about myself, and how does that drive my reactions and responses to a challenging situation? What are the facts and implications of the situation we are dealing with? What do I have control over that I can do something about? Let's dive into these three areas.

Step 1. Enhance Your Self-Awareness

What do I know about myself, and how does that drive my reactions and responses to a challenging situation?

The process begins with a self-awareness of what shapes your perspective. Factors such as your personality, values, life experiences, and emotional awareness all influence how you view and interact with the world around you. The better you understand yourself, the more equipped you are to shape your perspective of the crisis and a pathway to get through it.

To enhance self-awareness with my clients, I use a variety of personality, behavioral, and leadership assessments. This informs us as to the whys behind a person's leadership approach, and assists us in aligning the servant leadership and required organizational competencies to a more natural, authentic style.

The better you understand yourself, the more equipped you are to shape your perspective of the crisis and a pathway to get through it. #ResilienceReady

---

Let's consider five areas of self-awareness that significantly impact perspective.

- Personality and Behavioral Style
- Core Values
- Emotional Intelligence
- Experiences
- Authenticity

Personality and Behavioral Style

An assessment of your personality and behavioral style preferences gives you an indication of how you are typically most comfortable approaching a situation. Your personality is formed early in life around five common traits: openness to experiences, conscientiousness, extroversion, agreeableness, and neuroticism/emotional stability. Within those five traits are 32 characteristics that further define personality. These traits and characteristics, widely accepted within psychology, are reflected in a person's attitudes, beliefs, values, and behaviors. Behaviors are more fluid and are adapted based on external factors. Behavioral assessments often measure how you adapt your response and reactions to situations when under stress.

A person higher in introversion may deal with things more inward facing, relying on yourself, how you're feeling, and how you believe you can handle the situation. You are more introspective in dealing with a situation and are more comfortable trying to work it out on your own or with a small group of people. If you are higher in extraversion, you may be naturally more outgoing, reaching out and engaging others, feeling better able to get through a situation when you have a support system to help you.

Core Values

Your values system is the set of beliefs, principles, or standards around which you align your life, both personally and professionally.

Values develop over the course of your life and are influenced by the meaning you derive from your personal experiences and from observing the people and environment around you. Core values define what is most important to you and help you set priorities for your life. They influence your thought patterns and actions and represent characteristics by which you want to be known. "The good life sometimes has little to do with outside circumstances. We are happy and fulfilled mostly by who we are on the inside... And our internal lives largely contribute to producing many of our external circumstances," explains psychologist Dr. Henry Cloud in his *Success Magazine* article "10 Things Successful People Never Do Again."

Core values are like guardrails defining what is right for you; they assist you in making the many decisions you process in even a moment's time. They influence your worldview and how you respond in a crisis. A crisis can challenge your core values. Fear and anxiety brought on by a crisis can cause your thoughts, words, or actions to be out of alignment with your core values, creating inner tension and stress.

Core values are personal and sometimes unconscious. Your core values may include characteristics such as integrity, compassion, creativity, love, knowledge, learning, respect, kindness, honesty, curiosity, security, bravery, spirituality, service, and trust, among others.

Carmen Moreno-Rivera, Chief of Performance Improvement for Louisville, KY Metro Government, told me that her core values are the foundation for her self-awareness. Using a values sort exercise, she was able to prioritize what is most important to her. Facing tough challenges as a leader, especially during a crisis, she often revisits her core values to ensure her priorities, behaviors, and environment align with them. She suggests that you need time to reflect on how a crisis is affecting you and how you are responding.

Organizations also often identify core values, and apply them in much the same way as personal values. In order for organizational core values to be more than words on a poster, values must be communicated to and adopted by all employees. These shared values are ingrained in the culture and provide guidance in how organizations and the people in them behave and make decisions.

According to PwC's report, *The Human Side of Crisis,* "Our Global Crisis Survey confirms that two of the most important factors of an effective crisis response are teamwork and people sticking to the company's values: of those companies who self-identified as 'in a better place' post-crisis, huge majorities confirm that they acted with integrity and as a team." The study also found that "making values-based decisions can help bring the organization and its teams together, and come through the crisis stronger and more unified than before."

Consider This

Your Personal Values

What are your personal core values?
What role do your personal core values play in your leadership practice?
How do your personal core values align with your organization's core values?

(Complete the values sort exercise in the accompanying Resilience Ready Leader's Guide workbook.)

Emotional Intelligence

Emotional intelligence (EQ) is at the core of achieving personal effectiveness and interpersonal effectiveness with others.

"Emotional intelligence is the ability to sense, understand and effectively apply the power and acumen of your emotions and the emotions of others in order to facilitate higher levels of collaboration and productivity," according to TTI Success Insights. Daniel Goleman, internationally-known psychologist, pioneer in emotional intelligence research, and author of *Primal Leadership, Working with Emotional Intelligence,* among others, lays out four domains of emotional intelligence:

Personal Competence

- Self-Awareness — the ability to recognize and understand your emotions and how they influence your work and interactions with others
- Self-Management — the ability to control your emotions and behaviors

Social Competence

- Social Awareness — the ability to recognize the emotions of others and read organizational social constructs
- Relationship Management — the ability to constructively manage interactions and build relationships with others

Considering that performance at work is defined and judged based on behavioral observations, the importance of understanding and properly managing emotional energy becomes all the more important. Building your skill in emotional intelligence is even more critical as you move up in the organization. Leaders who use the language and practices of emotional intelligence cultivate an inclusive environment that can transform employee engagement, team collaboration, and business results.

Business leaders who use emotional intelligence to build an inclusive culture gain a competitive marketplace edge for their organization. Emotional intelligence can help you to be a resonant leader attuned with the emotions, concerns, and attitudes of yourself and your colleagues.

Emotional intelligence (EQ) is an integral part in determining how you lead. EQ impacts an organization's emotional climate and performance. Emotionally intelligent leaders are deliberate about engaging the most appropriate leadership approach for a given situation. The awareness of the situation, your emotions, others' emotions, and the potential implications are significant in evaluating needs and how best to engage. The challenge is to avoid an emotional hijack in how you approach a crisis, also engaging the pre-frontal neocortex area of the brain to make a more thoughtful response.

Experiences

When you're faced with a crisis, your mind will recall similar past experiences. You replay what you were able to learn from those experiences and what strategies and approaches seemed to work to get you through them. You also have an emotional connection to those past experiences. Were they positive and happy times in your life? Were they crises that incited anxiety and fear? Your immediate reaction will be to respond based on the memories those emotions resurface for you.

The more you are aware of what drives you during a crisis, and where you and your team stand emotionally, the better you will manage your response to lead and engage your team with a shift toward a more positive perspective.

Authenticity

When you know more about yourself and can use that insight to be more self-aware in situations, you will be more authentic in your leadership style. When you're in a crisis or an uncomfortable environment, the situation is outside of your normal day-to-day, and your human tendency is to shift your behavioral style. You move into a fight or flight mode, an emotional hijack in your brain ensues, and your behaviors reflect that natural response to survive.

In a crisis, that shift in your behavior becomes more evident. People who work with you can see the shift; your leadership is anxiety based, inauthentic. You try to look brave, but it's only a front.

"I believe when you're in a crisis, everybody goes to their default personality," explains Tonya Jackson. "The real you comes out. If people haven't seen that before, that's where teams get stuck. They may respond with 'what's wrong with her?' They don't know how to deal with you. Whatever your default personality is, it's going to ooze out in a crisis. Authenticity and trust are extremely important characteristics. Working through a crisis is easier if your team trusts you and they know the real you."

Authenticity also requires you to align your personal values with those of the organization. Being authentic helps you build trust in the working relationships with your team, a foundation that you will need to get through a crisis. Your team needs to be able to trust what you say and what you do. They need to trust that the decisions you make are in their best interest, even when tough decisions must be made and tough actions must be taken.

There is so much out of people's control during a crisis. They are looking to you for stability, reliability, and the genuine guidance and support to get through it.

Step 2. Take a Reality Check: Facts Over Fear

What are the facts and implications of the situation we are dealing with?

The next step in shifting your perspective is to gain some visual clarity about the crisis and its resulting implications. You need to describe your situation from a position of objectivity, rather than based on higher levels of emotion or bias that come from being in the middle of a situation.

In a crisis, you can fill your head with stories that are not based on reality. You have to take the opportunity to evaluate your current situation so that you can deal with the truth and find an appropriate path forward.

What steps can you take to get a more objective view?

1. Lay out the facts
2. Explore contributing factors
3. Assess the implications
4. Assess the degree of concern

Be sure to engage your team in the process. Welcome the diversity in the insights shared and conclusions drawn. The process will bring up good points for deeper discussion. The entire team will be well informed and better able to make data-based decisions.

Evaluate your current situation so that you can deal with the truth and find an appropriate path forward. #ResilienceReady

---

1. Lay Out the Facts

Your first step in evaluating your current situation is to lay out the facts. Separate the truths from opinions, propaganda, erroneous information, and rumors. Don't do this in a vacuum. Engage your team to bring forth the information they have and research relevant facts.

Questions you might ask include:

- What are the facts related to the overall crisis itself? What are we dealing with?
- What has been the impact outside of our business?
- What has been the impact on our organization?
- How are the facts and conditions evolving?

Create a process to keep information coming in so that you can make decisions based on the most current facts.

2. Explore Contributing Factors

Step two is to identify factors that are likely contributors to your current situation. Explore what may have contributed to the genesis of the crisis, as well as the current state of your organization within the crisis.

Questions you might ask include:

- What factors led to our ability and readiness to deal with the crisis?
- Reflecting back, what were some of the indicators of the crisis?
- How prepared were we for a crisis?
- What lessons have we learned?
- What steps could have been taken to further minimize the impact on our organization?

3. Assess the Implications

Step three is to assess what the impact of the crisis means for your organization. You're answering the question, "So what? What does this mean for us?" Consider the operational, financial, and human capital implications. Run scenarios to forecast what could happen if different events and responses unfold.

Questions you might ask include:

- What happened (or didn't happen) as a result of our current situation?
- How are our employees, customers, partners, and community dealing with the crisis, and what do they need?
- How can we quantify the operational, financial, and human capital impact?
- What are the short-term and longer-term implications based on what we anticipate happening in the future?

4. Assess the Degree of Concern

Step four is to assess the degree to which the implications from your analyses in step three are a concern. You want to prioritize potential risks and concerns, at which point you can determine appropriate action.

Questions you might ask include:

- Where are our greatest risks and concerns?
- Which risks are likely to have the greatest impact on the organization?

A risk analysis that considers the likelihood of occurrence versus the potential impact of each risk can be plotted using an x-y axis, two-by-two matrix, or nine-block matrix. The Failure Modes and Effects Analysis, a common tool used in Lean Six Sigma, additionally considers the potential severity of each risk and actions that can be taken to proactively mitigate or manage the resulting effects.

Consider This

Finding Helpful Resources

What resources might be useful in helping to evaluate the current situation and implications? Utilize economic data to understand the broad facts from a global, national, regional, state, and local level. Industry data can be secured from industry associations and other data sources to provide insight. Engage your customers to get direct feedback from them on how they are being impacted by the crisis, how they are responding, and how they need your partnership to get through this time (more on customer partnership in Chapter 8. Partnership.) Reach out to engage experts on pertinent topics and solutions.

Step 3. Power-Up Your Accountability

What do I have control over that I can do something about?

You may find yourself in the middle of a crisis feeling like there is nothing you can do. You have a choice. What you do, or don't do, will influence your outcomes in the short term and longer term.

You own your outcomes based on your perspective. #ResilienceReady

---

You can get through a crisis with a positive outcome if you decide you're going to be accountable for your perspective and how this turns out for you. With all the fear and elements out of your control, it's easy to be shut down and let others determine your outcome. When you are accountable, you focus on what you can do, the things you can control, versus everything that is outside of your control. Focusing on everything outside of your control creates overwhelm. You get stuck in the Victim Stage, Settled Stage, or Surviving Stage of internal crisis response. Your entire team becomes stuck.

You own your outcomes based on your perspective and how you react — powerless/do nothing or empowered to take advantage of the situation.

It's Time to Lead with a Positive Perspective!

Now that you have the facts and have evaluated the implications, you have more power to change your situation. Actions based on facts have a stronger likelihood to succeed. Be hopeful. Focus on the future you want to create. Stop looking in the rearview mirror and hoping for something different. Now you know the reality. You know what you're dealing with, and you've built a process to keep information flowing in, so you can monitor how the crisis evolves and respond with agility. You're mentally ready to forge ahead.

If you could use support getting yourself and/or your organization Resilience Ready, contact me at vivian@vivianblade.com.

Remember:

- → Your objective in this stage is to make a mental shift regarding the situation and possibilities.
- → Your outlook is heavily shaped by your surrounding environment.
- → The overflow of information instigates an emotional response that may not necessarily be a rational outlook on the situation.
- → A shift in perspective can be achieved through these three steps:
    - Step 1. Self-Awareness — What do I know about myself and how that drives my response/reaction to a challenging situation?
    - Step 2. A Reality Check — What are the facts and implications of the crisis situation?
    - Step 3. Accountability — What do I have control over that I can do something about?

Resilience Ready Today

Rapid Start Activity

PRINCIPLE 1. PERSPECTIVE

Goal: How can I use insights about myself and the realities of the crisis to be more accountable and make a mental shift regarding the situation and its possibilities?

Following are the most immediate reflections or actions that will get you on the path toward becoming a Resilience Ready Leader. Engage your team to inspire team resilience.

Step 1. Enhance Your Self-Awareness

Take Action

- **Take the right assessments** — Engage an executive coach or your HR partner for advice and to access appropriate assessments in areas where you need further insight. Assessments you should consider include: personality, behavioral style, motivations, emotional intelligence, stress, leadership style, 360° feedback, values sort, or strengths. Be open to the feedback. Reflect on experiences that will help you gain deeper insight. What are your "aha's?"
- **Apply what you've learned** — Most assessments provide suggestions on how to incorporate the feedback into your personal development. Outline specific action steps that will help you improve your interactions with others and strengthen authenticity in your leadership practice. An executive coach can help you personalize your action plan.
- **Make self-awareness a habit** — Get into a habit of asking for feedback and being reflective so you heighten your ongoing self-awareness and awareness in your interactions with others. Your executive coach can guide you in finding insights from the feedback and reflections. Periodically refresh the

assessments. Other assessments may also be recommended as you progress in your leadership journey.

Inspiring Team Resilience Discussion Questions

Take Action

- Download the Inspiring Team Resilience — Perspective Discussion Questions, and schedule time for discussions with your team. Visit https://ResilienceReady.today.

Resources

You may wish to use the accompanying *Resilience Ready Leader's Guide* workbook to complete these exercises. Additional resources also are available at https://ResilienceReady.today.

If you could use support with assessments and in taking action, contact me at vivian@vivianblade.com

Chapter 6

Purpose

RESILIENCE READY PRINCIPLE 2

"Change will not come if we wait for some other person or some other time. We are the ones we've been waiting for. We are the change that we seek." — Barack Obama

"Efforts and courage are not enough without purpose and direction." — John F. Kennedy

"In the heat of this situation, the urgency was obviously creating a lot of extra work for everyone," said Tim. "We quickly realized that not everyone had accurate information about what was going on with our supplier's fire, the resulting parts supply issues, and why we were taking certain steps. Priorities were shifting due to the need to reprioritize what we were working on for a while.

"This problem impacted everyone's work in some way. Some of our team members were working on immediate actions that were needed to manage the most pressing issues. Other team members were focused on more long-term projects to put future mitigation processes in place. Another group was developing new services we learned we could help our current and new customers with.

"This crisis created some longer-term changes for us that were frankly pretty exciting. We could go in a number of different directions. So, we had to be clear on what we were trying to accomplish and the vision of the future we wanted for our company. My boss, Kayla, had us spend time working with our teams to define what we wanted the future to look like for us after this fiasco. The mission and vision for our company ultimately didn't change. But we were able to reframe our purpose for getting through this time and beyond based on the challenges we needed to address and the opportunities that came out of it.

"We had been going along doing what we always do, manufacturing component parts for our tech industry customers, using the same partners and processes we had been using for years. We had an opportunity to work differently and to expand our market to new industries by aligning with new partners. For all this to work, we had to make sure our team was bought in. We spent time with individual team members to first listen to their concerns and ideas, and to find out from them how they wanted to plug in to create our future vision. There was a lot of work ahead, and we had to make sure that we engaged employees every step of the way."

Why Purpose Is Important to Achieving Resilience

Because of the chaos during challenging times, people can get caught up in fighting fires and adjusting to change. You shift into survival mode, both as individuals and as an organization. Different priorities emerge and seem to shift day-to-day, week-to-week. The work volume increases. There's a lot of worry and chatter, all of which can make it difficult to focus on what's most important.

Staying focused has never been more critical than in times of crisis.

Your challenge is to create a meaningful future instead of falling victim to "however this turns out." #ResilienceReady

Purpose gives meaning to our existence as human beings. Purpose in a crisis is shaped by the role you play as both a leader and an organization as you move through the crisis, and manifests in a vision of who you will be as you emerge from the crisis.

Your challenge is to create a meaningful future instead of falling victim to "however this turns out." What are we destined to do? Who are we destined to be? How are we being called to serve?

Purpose is fueled by a vision beyond adversity. Let's go back to the train analogy. If you're riding the train and don't know where you're going, you can't imagine when the journey will end; if you stay on until the end of the ride, what will be at the end? Will it be positive or negative? Will it be what you wanted or expected? Where will you be, and how in the world will you get home? Riding the train without an idea of where you'll end up is worrisome, exhausting, and stressful.

If you face a crisis in the same manner, you will flounder and lose the ability to accomplish your greatest potential. You'll be unable to sustain your operations, because you'll be constantly reacting to the situation instead of taking control of it. The journey will be worrisome, exhausting, and stressful, not only for the leaders, but for everyone involved.

Purpose gives you direction, guidance, and hope, all of which are needed to overcome a crisis. You can make the decisions for who and what you want to be on the other side of a crisis. You may not have all the answers for how to get there right now, but as you move forward, the steps will illuminate.

Purpose gives you direction, guidance, and hope, all of which are needed to overcome a crisis. #ResilienceReady

Resilience is discovered in the comforting confidence of a meaningful purpose and hopeful future.

How a Crisis Impacts Purpose

During a crisis, purpose can be foggy. You may lose your sense of purpose because you don't know what to expect. You can't see what's ahead. You feel a lack of control because you don't know what the journey will bring, so you try to take it one step at a time as you determine your next move. You know that you need that purpose for a sense of direction to guide your path forward, otherwise you're not sure where you'll end up. Your purpose may slightly shift based on others' needs from you. For organizations the shift may initiate from changes in how customers, industry, and the communities you serve need you during and after a crisis.

Your current purpose may be in greater demand during a crisis, bringing clarity to what you are called to do. Grocery stores and food/household staple manufacturers were a lifeline during the COVID-19 pandemic. Companies that fulfilled this need were considered essential businesses like no other time in their existence.

During the September 11, 2001 attacks on the United States, as the hijacked planes destroyed buildings and lives in New York, Virginia, and Pennsylvania, first responders didn't hesitate in fulfilling their purpose to do their best to save lives. Day in and day out, first responders and our military go without hesitation into unknown, dangerous situations, many sacrificing their own lives for others'.

Consequences When Purpose Lacks Meaning

Nackia Salmon shares how purpose has become even more important to her: "It's the funerals that I've been attending. Over the years as some people get older all you hear is regret… regretting so much more of what they didn't do. I think my grandmother did not see herself as being empowered to be intentional about her choices. She was strong because she survived. But she stayed being a survivor, being a victim, not thriving. So, having greater self-perception, greater self-worth and value, knowing herself, and having intention about how she lived her life… she didn't. She stayed in survival mode and died mentally in survival mode and never really had joy. When you come to my funeral, it will be a celebration. Even if it's tomorrow, it's going to be rich, because I have made intentional changes to make sure that whatever time I've been given so far, I have done well with it."

When you lack meaningful purpose for your life, you risk experiencing a journey of survival and regret. You spend years surviving, missing the joy that manifests from your service to the world when you thrive. And the world misses out on the potential you have to give.

The same holds true for organizations when purpose is hollow of meaning. There's nothing for leaders or their teams to connect to, either personally or professionally. Because a crisis creates chaos and different work to be done, employees are confused about what they are supposed to do. They lose focus. They're stretched thin with more to do and less time to do it. Productivity suffers. Depending on the environment surrounding the crisis, employees' time may be at a higher premium, so lacking a purpose to guide their priorities results in wasted time, higher labor costs, and missed opportunities. Employees also feel the chaos and don't feel like they're spending their energy on meaningful work. They can feel like their talent is wasted, and you risk higher employee turnover.

When you lack meaningful purpose for your life, you risk experiencing a journey of survival and regret. #ResilienceReady

---

Advantages of Meaningful Purpose

"It's not enough to have lived. We should be determined to live for something." — Winston S. Churchill

Purpose breeds focus and energy, giving you a place to direct your attention. We need purpose for fulfillment and to feel like we're doing meaningful work and making a difference in the world. Purpose aligns with the fourth level of Maslow's Hierarchy of Needs, which demonstrates that people need a sense of accomplishment in order to fulfill their esteem needs. This especially holds true as generational workplace trends shift, with professionals expecting that their career serves a meaningful purpose.

Purpose has a direct operational impact. Your team will be in a better position to deliver solid operating results when everyone is on the same page, aligned toward the same goals. "Companies with a strong mission and purpose outperformed the S&P 500 by 8-fold over a 20 year period," according to the Deloitte study, *The Future of Work: The People Imperative.*

Purpose breeds focus and energy. #ResilienceReady

Steps to Becoming Resilience Ready

Steps to Reframe Your Purpose

You may be like many people who struggle with knowing the purpose for their life. You may find yourself in a job that draws a paycheck but doesn't feed your soul. Often, the belief is that purpose has to be some grand statement about your life, much like a corporate mission and vision statement. While we can use those as examples, most important is that your purpose speaks to your heart and comes from your passion and the contributions you can make to the world. John Lewis, U.S. Congressman and civil rights leader, said it well in his essay, *Together, You Can Redeem the Soul of Our Nation,* published in *The New York Times* just after his death: "Though I am gone, I urge you to answer the highest calling of your heart and stand up for what you truly believe."

As an organization, your purpose is commonly defined through your mission statement, your reason for being, and your vision statement, which reflects the impact you wish to make in the world. Your mission and vision help you align your team and your resources to what you are striving to become. Your challenge as a leader is to make sure these are not just words on paper, but rather they come to life in your everyday commitments, investments, behaviors and actions.

Your purpose must come to life in your everyday commitments, investments, behaviors, and actions. #ResilienceReady

Your purpose is your North Star, which also guides your personal decisions and actions. Because of the evolving needs during a crisis, your personal and/or organizational purpose may need to be reframed in response to the current situation.

The following steps will guide you in renewing or reframing your purpose:

Step 1. Create a ***vision beyond the adversity***
Step 2. Establish ***clear priorities***
Step 3. Align your ***resources***

Step 1. Create a Vision Beyond the Adversity

Re-examine Your Why

In a situation such as a national or global crisis, needs shift to a societal scale. Therefore, your purpose is likely to shift in the short term. You may get back to your core mission, but even that will likely be adjusted as you move through the crisis. A new reality is often set. What is your purpose in that new reality? How might you adapt to meet the needs of the current situation and anticipated future environment?

During a crisis, purpose needs to be clearer and stronger than ever, both for yourself and for others. Clarity in organizational purpose helps not only executives make decisions, but it also helps employees make decisions about their day-to-day work. Employees can take part in reshaping your purpose to get the best ideas and to grow commitment for the difficult journey ahead.

You can't reframe your purpose in isolation. Being unified means coming together to co-create the future. You've probably heard the saying "two heads are better than one." When you bring in collective wisdom and ideas, greater possibilities can emerge. Personally, you may engage your family, your innermost circle, and other experts in exploring how the situation has shifted and where attention is needed. Observe the intersection of those needs and what you are most passionate about. What role can you play in finding solutions and serving others?

Engage employees in reshaping your purpose to get the best ideas and to grow commitment for the difficult journey ahead. #ResilienceReady

In your leadership role, engage your employees and customers to help refine your purpose based on re-examining how the world has changed and how it needs you right now. Engage your team to define your possibilities based on what you learn. There will be greater buy-in because team members take ownership of what they want and what the future holds.

The key questions to address are: What outcomes and future state are we working toward? How can we emerge from this adversity even stronger?

If you can see a hopeful future beyond the adversity, you can generate energy that inspires you to take action and momentum from taking action toward your stronger future state.

Consider This

How did your purpose shift during the most recent crisis you experienced... personally/professionally/organizationally?

Reassess Customer Needs

We are rarely more fulfilled than when we can do something to help others. Your customers will appreciate your reaching out in true concern for their well-being. How can you use your resources, intellect, and technology to answer a calling?

During the COVID-19 pandemic many companies used their strengths to answer a pressing need for the country. There was a need for personal protective equipment for healthcare workers and essential front line-workers. Spirits companies switched from making bourbon to making hand sanitizer. They were able to use their equipment, supplies, processes, and knowledge to shift what they were making, fulfilling a critical need. Manufacturers and schools were able to take 3-D printing machines and plastics that would normally be used to produce appliances and other equipment to manufacture face shields for health care workers and partitions to be used in all types of applications, from grocery stores to restaurants, banks, and offices.

Assess the Economic Environment & Industry

Most crises don't come out of nowhere. There's been a turn of events over time that impact the economic environment globally, nationally, industry-wide, and, ultimately, within your company.

Your industry is changing around you. You've got to be aware of how a crisis reshapes industry norms.

- How are regulations changing?
- Where are new opportunities emerging in the industry?
- Who struggled during the crisis, leaving gaps in unmet needs?
- Where has competitive advantage shifted to?
- How can your organization take the lead in innovation?
- Have new markets opened up as a result of the crisis?
- How have technology trends shifted?
- Where do you need to invest?

Technology shifts provide vivid examples of how industries are driven to rapid change. Technology has permeated nearly every aspect of our lives, both personally and within organizations. In the grocery and restaurant industries, online ordering, curbside pickup, and home delivery became commonplace in a relatively short time. The COVID-19 pandemic accelerated this shift when consumer demand changed. Amazon's conversion of its fleet of trucks and vans to electric powered vehicles fulfills their purpose of zero carbon emissions to help the environment.

Seek reliable information sources. Team members can do some research and information gathering to better understand the new landscape. Reach out to your industry association to gather insights from their research and connections across the industry.

As you gather and assess the incoming information, consider the implications specifically for your organization. What is the short-term impact? What are the longer-term implications?

As you evaluate how your purpose should align going forward, proceed with caution. You don't want to stray far from your core business. That's your strength, your competitive advantage. You do, however, need to become knowledgeable about the challenges your customers and industry are dealing with, and how you may be a resource.

Step 2. Establish Clear Priorities

A recent visit to the eye doctor revealed that as another year passed, my eyesight got worse. I'm going to need a stronger eyeglass prescription to read clearly. When I'm not wearing my glasses, or when the words are too small, it's not only difficult to read, but it impacts my ability to focus and comprehend reading material. I'm squinting (as I find myself doing now while writing this), and my brain is more focused on just trying to see, rather than absorbing what I'm reading.

Seeing Clearly

Your view is often blurry as you go through a crisis. You can't clearly see the future or everything going on around you. You could use reading glasses to help bring clarity and focus.

During a crisis, different priorities emerge. More of the focus is on fighting fires, taking care of the most urgent, pressing challenges you face. That doesn't necessarily mean all of the other work disappears. Generally more is added to everyone's plate, both personally and professionally. Clarity of purpose helps you determine where you will focus your time and energy, what you will say "yes" or "no" to. Be sure to establish clear personal, professional, and organizational priorities based on the reframing of your purpose during these times. Employees are seeking solid and clear guidance. They need your direction on what must be done by when, and which tasks should take a back seat to others. However, don't mistake this for micromanaging.

Clarity of purpose helps you determine where you will focus your time and energy, what you will say "yes" or "no" to. #ResilienceReady

---

How you work may be different for some time. During a crisis, people may take on different roles. As with the COVID-19 crisis, employees were working remotely, with many other family responsibilities to manage, such as schooling for their children. Employees also need clarity in expectations for work arrangements, deliverables, and deadlines. Identify where employees need support in order to get work done. There may be barriers you need to move for them, or resources you need to make available for them to complete their work.

Clear priorities improve purpose and productivity.

Step 3. Align Your Resources

Communicating Purpose

Passion lies with purpose. When purpose and priorities adjust during a crisis, communication is critical. First communicate the factors which caused the need for adjustment. Let employees know that they are helping to reshape the purpose; engage them early on and let them know how they will be a part of the process.

As the purpose adjusts, develop a communication plan for employees, customers, and all stakeholders that explains why and how adjustments have been made. How did each stakeholder group play a role? What part will each stakeholder play in fulfilling your purpose? What does the purpose mean for each stakeholder group and each individual represented? Help them to understand.

Make It Personal

It's impossible for employees or customers to support the organization's purpose without feeling a personal connection to it. Therefore, it is critical to first discover individual purpose. One of the main reasons employees leave their jobs after having an inadequate

---

Employees leave their jobs because they are missing a connection to both personal and professional purpose. #ResilienceReady

---

manager is they don't feel their work is meaningful. They're missing a connection to both professional and personal purpose. The larger the organization, the harder it becomes to make this connection at all levels.

Helping employees discover their own purpose and connecting that to the company's purpose takes one-on-one time to discuss what is important to them, the value they bring, and their individual goals.

Approach these conversations like a coaching discussion, where you are not giving answers, but asking questions that help guide toward self-discovery.

- When you think about your work, what is most important to you? What are you passionate about? What would make you most proud? If money were no object, what type of work would you do?
- Why did you decide to work for us?
- What has been rewarding about your work here so far? What has been frustrating?
- What are some of your skills that you consider strengths? Which of your skills do you feel are not being fully utilized?
- What accomplishments are you most proud of?
- How do you believe you could best contribute as we go through this crisis?
- Describe what work fulfillment would look like.
- Given how the environment around us has changed as a result of this crisis, how should the purpose of this organization adjust?
- What role do you believe you can play in helping us fulfill our purpose?

Work with employees to find the strongest points of connection and find ways to involve them in the related work, either as part of their normal job responsibilities or as a special assignment.

Realign Your Talent

In order to fulfill your purpose, you must consider your environment during and coming out of a crisis. The purpose you need to fulfill in the short term and longer term will affect the skill set you need on your team. A crisis usually brings about significant change and the need to adapt to what is required of you. You've got a lot invested in your current workforce. Assess your talent needs, capabilities, and gaps.

Invest in upskilling, reskilling, and developing your workforce to close those gaps. Often companies will pull back on expenses during a crisis. If you take a scarcity view and forgo investing in your capabilities to sustain and return to growth, you'll find your company behind and struggling to survive. AT&T realized nearly half its workforce of 250,000 employees did not have the necessary skills for the company to remain competitive and committed to investing $1 billion to retrain employees for jobs of the future.

Focused energy on the needs related to the crisis may require the creation of new work teams whose mission and day-to-day responsibilities are addressing the crisis, while other employees remain focused on your core business. Ensure these teams have the financial, material, and human resources to complete their charge.

Taking Tough Action with Humanity

Realigning your talent may mean that layoffs and furloughs are inevitable during a crisis. These are tough decisions that must be made, especially when you have a highly talented team.

Beyond the regulatory considerations with these types of actions, ensure you are using objective, unbiased criteria to make decisions about who will be affected. If your selections are purported to be "performance" based, have you done everything you reasonably could to help each individual succeed? Have you been considerate of the challenges that individuals are facing (sometimes beyond their control) due to the crisis? Is a particular group of employees impacted more so than others? Why is that the case? Do your policies and practices (official and unofficial) include hidden biases, whether or not intentional? Take a good hard look at the implications of your decisions before taking action.

Through this process you need to consider not only how to have the conversations with those affected employees, but also those who remain. Rumors and anxiety can escalate across your entire workforce.

The parting will be painful and emotional. There are so many other stressors people are dealing with, so make sure you take that into consideration as you plan your discussions. Help employees understand why the actions are being taken and what to expect. Let them know that their contributions to the company are valued. Keep them as whole as possible.

Consider This

Going Through a Layoff or Furlough?

Leading Employees Transitioning Out

How do you help employees transition out when their shortened careers may not be by choice?

1. Be as transparent as possible.
2. Appreciate them.
3. Be empathetic to their emotions and concerns; listen.
4. Share resources for next steps.
5. Give the space and bandwidth needed to transition out, where the situation permits.

Leading the Remaining Team

How do you handle the aftermath and coming days with the remaining employees?

1. What assurances can you give?
2. Be as transparent as possible.
3. Appreciate them.
4. Be empathetic to their emotions and concerns; listen.
5. Make yourself available for employees to come to you with concerns.
6. Provide direction.

(You can catch Vivian's full article "Leading Through a Layoff" at https://ResilienceReady.today)

It's Time to Lead with Purpose!

You can't get through a crisis without a clear and meaningful purpose for yourself, and one that is connected at an organizational and individual level. You generate energy and momentum by having a direction to work toward.

Your purpose as leader is to be like a reliable lighthouse during the storm, supporting your team in illuminating a meaningful path forward to achieving the purpose. The facilitator role helps get through the crisis both as individuals and as a team.

Remember:

→ Your challenge is to create a meaningful future instead of falling victim to "however this turns out." What are we destined to do? Who are we destined to be? How are we being called to serve?

→ Resilience is discovered in the comforting confidence of a meaningful purpose and hopeful future.

→ In your leadership role, engage your employees and customers in helping to refine your purpose based on re-examining how the world has changed and how it needs you right now.

→ The following steps will guide you in renewing or reframing your purpose:

- Step 1. Create a purpose beyond the adversity
- Step 2. Establish clear priorities
- Step 3. Align your resources

Resilience Ready Today

Rapid Start Activity

PRINCIPLE 2. PURPOSE

Goal: How are we being called to serve? What outcomes and future state are we working toward? How can we emerge from this adversity even stronger?

Following are the most immediate reflections or actions that will get you on the path toward becoming a Resilience Ready Leader. Engage your team to inspire team resilience.

Step 1. Create a Vision Beyond the Adversity

Reflections

- Consider the current crisis you are experiencing. By the end of the crisis, describe how you envision your well-being (i.e., emotional, physical, spiritual, financial, etc.). Looking back, what will you be most proud of?

  You may also complete this activity considering a recent past crisis. What would you have envisioned?

Inspiring Team Resilience Discussion Questions

Take Action

- Download the Inspiring Team Resilience — Purpose Discussion Questions and schedule time to have discussions with your team. Visit https://ResilienceReady.today.

Resources

You may wish to use the accompanying *Resilience Reader Leader's Guide* workbook to complete these exercises. Additional resources also are available at https://ResilienceReady.today.

If you could use support with assessments and in taking action, contact me at vivian@vivianblade.com

CHAPTER 7

Perseverance

RESILIENCE READY PRINCIPLE 3

"When you get into a tight place and everything goes against you...never give up then, for that is just the place and time that the tide will turn."
— Harriet Beecher Stowe

"If there is no struggle, there is no progress."
— Frederick Douglass

"Success is to be measured not so much by the position that one has reached in life as by the obstacles which [one] has overcome while trying to succeed."
— Booker T. Washington

"A week into the crisis and everybody was already worn out," recalls Tim. "We'd been scrambling just trying to keep our heads above water. We hadn't been through a crisis of this same scale before. So, we were sometimes figuring things out as we went along. It felt quite chaotic a lot of the time. I began to see how stressed everyone was becoming. Because everything was moving so fast and we were so busy, it was tough to keep good information flowing. We later realized that we weren't communicating often enough and employees were beginning to distrust us leaders. Rumors were beginning to spread, which was escalating the stress even more.

"Kayla regrouped the leadership team and pulled in members of the communications team to help us put together and implement a communication plan. We got clear on the needs for sharing information among our employees and other stakeholders. We made sure each communication was purposeful, provided as much relevant information as we knew or could share at the time, and included the 'why' behind some decisions being made.

"We also made room for plenty of feedback and listening so we could understand what employees and customers were hearing and feeling, what they were concerned about, the level of stress at any given time, and how we could best support them through this. We provided stress management resources during the workday and beefed up our employee assistance program with these services.

"Kayla also put together a core crisis response team who could focus full time on vetting options, planning, and coordinating the resources and implementation of our crisis response plan. They were great about involving all types of groups, both internal and external to the company, to evaluate our options, determine our best course of action and what needed to be done. We all had to be agile, as this was pretty complex and things were changing so fast. But, we knew with a good plan, organized structure, and willingness to hang in there together supporting each other, even though we'd have many rough patches along the way, we would be able to persevere through this."

Why Perseverance Is Important to Achieving Resilience

When you hear the stories of climbers on expeditions to the summit of Mt. Everest, the world's tallest mountain, it's hard to imagine what the expedition is like. They face grueling conditions along the way, and not just with the climb itself; imagine climbing through conditions of temperatures below zero degrees and a scarcity of oxygen over the several days it takes to get to the summit and back. The risks include possible snowstorms and avalanches, hypothermia and cardiovascular issues, and even death. The preparation required for these climbs takes months, if not years.

One of the most incredible stories of perseverance comes from an amputee, Charlie Linville, whose attempts to climb Mt. Everest in 2016 were chronicled in both the *Boston Globe* and *Washington Post*. The story reports Charlie as "the first person to reach the 29,035-foot summit with a prosthetic." Author of the article, Yanan Wang, writes, "The journey and its successful conclusion were a testament to human resilience against all odds."

By persevering through a challenge, you can physically reverse the inertia that can trap you when you lack control. #ResilienceReady

By persevering through a challenge, you can physically reverse the inertia that can trap you when you lack control. Like an expedition to a mountain summit, when going through a crisis there's a lot out of your control. When you're in tough conditions and lack control, you can feel hopeless, helpless, and unable to make it through. Perseverance gives you the psychological, emotional, and physical strength to push through the adversity regardless of what you have to face. The journey is arduous. You've got to have the inner will to keep going.

Perseverance is nonexistent without Perspective and Purpose, resilience principles 1 and 2, which give you the psychological foundation that you can overcome and that it's worth the struggle. #ResilienceReady

Perseverance is nonexistent without Perspective and Purpose, resilience principles 1 and 2, which give you the psychological foundation that you can overcome and that it's worth the struggle. These principles provide inspiration to take on the tough times ahead.

How a Crisis Impacts Perseverance

Sure, you plan for risks and crisis management within your company. But many of the crises you face are often unexpected, you don't see them coming, or at least you don't expect the timing. Often, one challenge after another seem to pile on top of each other. You can't get ahead before another event occurs. During hurricanes, heavy rain causes severe flooding in already vulnerable communities. How in the world could residents possibly get through all that?

Getting through a crisis is a tough slog. You feel like giving up. You're tired. You wish life and business would get back to how it used to be, what you were accustomed to. It's hard to keep going when it feels like you take one step forward and two steps back. Fear and setbacks tell you that you can't do it, you can't make it, so you might as well give up.

It's hard to ignore the voice inside your head, and even others who sing the refrain of impossibility, when it seems to be coming from all directions so loud and clear.

Do you remember learning to ride a bike once the training wheels came off? My brother Elbert helped me learn to ride. He would help me get steady and then give me a little push to get going. Until I got a feel for how to balance myself, I fell several times. I ended up with a few scraped elbows and knees, but I really wanted to learn to ride. So, even though it hurt, I would pick my bike up and try it again. I'd beg my brother to take me out again the next day to help me get back on that bike.

This is a simple example of perseverance most of us can relate to. Though the stakes are pretty low in learning to ride a bike, this demonstrates the spirit with which we need to go into a crisis. Give it a try, get back up, brush off and try again. A fall often doesn't hurt as bad as you scare yourself into believing, and you fall far less often than you expect.

Consequences When Fear Overtakes the Will to Persevere

Imagine yourself standing at the base of Mt. Everest getting ready to begin your expedition to the summit. You look up and you can't even see it. You just see an enormous snow-capped mountain range covered by clouds. You feel a pit in your stomach and your mind asks you, "Who do you think you are? Do you really believe you can make it to the top? What if something goes wrong? Look at the steep incline and all that snow? What if there's an avalanche? What if you don't have enough oxygen? Did you really prepare enough? Do you have all the right equipment you need? Some people don't make it back. Is it worth the risk?"

Now you're even more nervous. You feel this pit in your stomach as beads (no, streams) of sweat break out above your brow. Your view of the mountain before you is that it is just too big and too dangerous to believe you could possibly make it. You're ready to throw in the towel, even after all the hard work, time, and expense to get here.

When you look into the eyes of a crisis, you see a giant mountain in front of you that you couldn't possibly imagine climbing up, going around, or getting through. You lose hope and confidence. When your will to persevere is low, fear and lack of confidence can create despair, because you see no way through. You risk being stagnant, doing nothing or very little because you don't think it will make a difference anyway. When you do nothing you lose ground, get behind. You begin to feel defeated.

When teams experience that sense of despair, morale and productivity suffer. Your team can get stuck in this place. Instead of swimming ahead, employees are just treading water waiting for the shark to pass. They have a false sense of security. They fail to realize that their splashing water is getting the shark's attention, and their problem is about to get a lot worse.

Operating results suffer when your team is stuck in the Victim Stage or Settled Stage of internal crisis response. Your will to persevere is drained. You lose your competitive edge, resulting in lost opportunities and lost revenue. You can't see the opportunities emerging around you. You try to hold on to what has been, to what you are today, instead of facing reality and persevering ahead.

Operating results suffer when your team is stuck in the Victim Stage or Settled Stage. #ResilienceReady

Advantages When Perseverance Overtakes Fear

"I am lucky that whatever fear I have inside me, my desire to win is always stronger." — Serena Williams

Your drive to keep going flows from a deep willpower inside of you. You will have setbacks along the way, but you find that if you don't stop and keep trying, you can push through the barriers as they rear their ugly heads. Even the small successes build on each other, giving you momentum to make it to the next milestone.

Persevering through a crisis reminds me of those race car video games. You have a limited amount of time to make it through the course and earn as many points as you can. As you play, obstacles seemingly appear out of nowhere. You've got to react quickly, but not too wildly or you'll wreck and the game will end; so you do your best to keep your eyes glued to the road, gripping the steering wheel tight while you anticipate the obstacles that you know will appear. As you psych yourself up to handle the obstacles, you suddenly crash into a wall, quickly get back on the track, and accelerate toward the finish line.

Teams that persevere together have a common experience in the struggles they face and the triumphs they achieve. Colleagues pull together to support each other. It's the strength of working together and honoring one another through a crisis that brings the team together.

When your team works together to persevere through the struggles, team morale strengthens, productivity increases, and operating results improve. You're in a better position to support customers, who will reward you in long-term loyalty. Teams persevering together increase the sense of hope and energy. Each individual experiences a community strength that is unavailable when you go it alone.

As you break through each barrier, the path becomes clearer and new opportunities present themselves that you couldn't see before, or that weren't there.

Steps to Becoming Resilience Ready

Steps to Strengthen Perseverance

"Failure is only the opportunity to begin again, this time more intelligently." — Henry Ford

We can learn from mountain climbers that perseverance requires the following:

Step 1. Setting the stage for the environment in which you will operate, optimizing your chances to make it through seemingly impossible conditions.

Step 2. Roadmapping your path forward by planning and preparing for the expedition, physical, emotional and psychological conditioning, ensuring you have the right resources and equipment, engaging the right partners, laying out contingency plans, and practicing on a smaller scale.

Step 3. Taking decisive action, actually making the climb, grueling step-by-step, elevation-by-elevation, constantly scanning and assessing the changing conditions, and being agile to adjust as required.

You can apply a similar approach to persevering as you lead through a crisis.

Step 1. Set the Environment

You can't always control the conditions in which the crisis exists, but you can set the environment in which you operate through it. The environment reflects the culture of the team and the organization. Leaders establish the environment based around personal values and the organization's values, principles, and practices. A crisis automatically brings tension. If not managed effectively, that tension can lead to lack of trust, strained working relationships, a stressful climate, negativity, and poor results. Managed effectively, the tension can bring

Effectively setting a constructive environment and guiding your team through adversity takes perseverance that is grounded in the leadership practices of transparency and deep courage. #ResilienceReady

the team together to build trust, strengthen working relationships, foster an empathetic and inclusive climate, and offer hope, empowerment, and growth.

Effectively setting a constructive environment and guiding your team through adversity takes perseverance that is grounded in the leadership practices of transparency and deep courage.

Transparency & Trust

If you want your team and your customers to be in the game with you, transparency is non-negotiable. How should you approach transparency?

There's a lot of misinformation swirling around, especially during a crisis. Misinformation and rumors come from all directions. People don't know who to trust. Employees and customers are looking to leaders for honesty.

Truth brings about calm and commitment because you give the team a better understanding about what is happening and what to expect. They can trust you to be honest with them, whether it's good news or bad. Put yourself in the shoes of an employee who is in the dark without accurate information, not knowing what is going to happen next. How is the company going to handle this? Am I going to lose my job? How am I going to support my family?

I recall a few times when the companies I worked for were going through a merger or acquisition. The first question employees had was whether or not the acquisition rumor was true. There were many conversations going on behind closed doors. There was a lot of information that legally couldn't be shared, but people didn't have the patience for that, and the rumors were rampant. Employees were chattering and had anxiety about what the merger would mean for their jobs. They wondered how the culture would change and how their day-to-day would be affected. There was often more silence than communication during those times, which caused suspicion.

Though everything is moving so fast, it's worth the time investment to develop a communication plan specifically for employees, customers, and other stakeholders. "Set a time each week to meet with members of your team to give up-to-date information about the crisis or opportunity," recommends John Hackett. People need information, such as what the situation is, the implications of the situation (what does that mean for us), and the actions you're taking to get through the challenges, to serve their needs, and to keep them safe. They need direction on what's next, what they should be doing, and how they can help. Create a culture of transparency where connecting and sharing information is fluid within teams, across teams, with customers, and with partners.

[The CRISP communication model is ideal for communicating with transparency and for building trust. Check out the diagram in the "Consider This" section below.]

Consider This

CRISP Communication Model

How might a communication model such as this be beneficial for your organization to communicate with greater transparency and build trust?

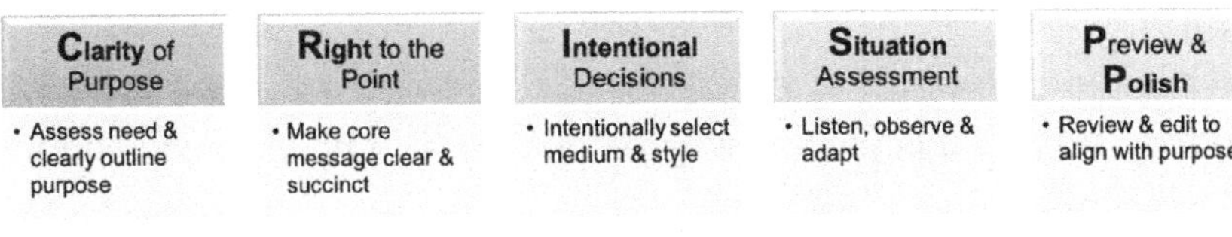

©Vivian Blade

Even when you don't have all the answers, share what you know. When there is information you can't yet share, let people know that as well. Tell them it's not ready to be released. "Here's what we know now"; "Here are the decisions still in progress."

Some decisions may not be universally popular. It's helpful to provide rationale for why decisions are being made. Make space for questions and concerns, and respond with empathy. Be truthful, despite having good or bad news. Lay out the facts. Reassure where you can, but, be careful not to stretch or sugarcoat the truth, or to over promise. If a person knows what they're dealing with, and who they're dealing with, they trust that they can work through the challenges and move forward.

When practiced as a core value, transparency will strengthen trust and commitment. Trust can build much needed community during tough times.

Courage

FEAR is all around you. The constant reports and rumors of worsening conditions, and some of the hard actions you have to take, create anxiety. You're left feeling worried, hopeless, and helpless.

As a leader responsible both for guiding your team and still getting work done, the road ahead is emotional, frightening, and uncertain. Even the toughest may not want to admit how vulnerable they feel during these times. You are embarrassed to let others see that you're nervous, too. You put on a brave face, but inside you feel like an imposter. You're expected to be cool, confident, and have all the answers.

Getting through this crisis will take courage. But how do you find it?

- Face your FEAR
- Reframe your stress
- Take a calculated step forward

Face Your FEAR

A wise mentor and friend, Ray Gazaway recently encouraged me to be resilient in facing my fear. He reminded me of the familiar saying, **F**alse **E**vidence **A**ppearing **R**eal, and said that "we have to be willing to pull back the curtain on fear." When you face a crisis, all you see is what is on the surface and the stories you tell yourself about what you think you see or hear. Think about your favorite murder mystery book or movie. It takes some digging to get to the facts about the crime.

You also have to dig beneath the surface information to find the realities of a crisis. Once you do, you'll have a clearer perspective on the situation. You can specifically identify what concerns you and why. You'll reveal "false evidence" you were falsely worried about. You can deal more directly with the realities and their effects. Keep in mind that you're not helpless as you face the truths. Shift your attention to things you can control, which begins with your perspective and focus. You'll discover greater confidence and realize that you have more control than you thought over managing outcomes.

Reframe Your Stress

Others can tell when you're stressed or uneasy, even though you try to hide it. Your goal is to reframe that stress so that you can reduce the anxiety and find the energy to work your way through your situation. It's important to be aware of your stress level and how it impacts your overall well-being.

How can you reframe your stress and frustration and use it to generate positive energy, rather than depleted energy?

Your first step is to recognize your stress and its contributing factors. Stress can affect your health, your work, and your relationships. How does it affect you? The fact that you are facing a crisis, and the innate response from your brain to try and protect you, can initiate stress. Stressors often come from the volume of work, work hours, and expectations that increase during a crisis. Uncertainty may cause you to worry, which can also bring on stress.

Using a stress assessment instrument to help individuals gauge their stress levels and contributors is an ideal starting point for awareness and healing. As a leader, you can check in with individuals, and the team can explore ways to reduce or eliminate contributing factors.

All kinds of emotions surface when you are in a crisis situation, and can vary as you go through different stages of a crisis; fear, anxiety, overwhelm, hopelessness, hopefulness, anger, blame, excitement, compassion... the list goes on. You want to become more self-aware of the emotions that appear during a crisis situation and allow yourself to let those emotions surface; then name the emotions and write them down, so you can face and release them. When you ignore, hide, or push down your emotions, the stress is exacerbated. Periodically check in with yourself to identify the emotion and assess how the stress from that emotion affects you.

Using a stress assessment instrument to help individuals gauge their stress levels and contributors is an ideal starting point for awareness and healing.
#ResilienceReady

Consider This

Which emotions surface for you when going through a crisis? How has the stress from those emotions affected you?

(The accompanying Resilience Ready Leader's Guide workbook includes exercises and resources to assist you in reframing your stress.)

You can also reframe your stress by reframing the negative self-talk you beat yourself up with. When you are in FEAR, your brain kicks in with a primitive survival response from all of the stories that the situation's first impressions tell you. Before you know it, your mind is repeating statements to you about your lack of capability to handle the crisis. Again, you want to be aware of and write down these statements so that you can face and release them. What are some of the negative statements you say to yourself in challenging situations? Practice restating those negative thoughts as positive affirmations about your capabilities.

Purpose and perspective are strong contributors to reframing your stress. When those emotions bring on stress, take 60 seconds to close your eyes, breathe slowly, and refocus on your *purpose* and a hopeful *perspective*.

When you begin to tense up, breathing is one of the best strategies to calm down. When you're anxious, your heart races and your breathing hastens. If you can, close your eyes and try to reconnect with your breathing. Move your breathing down into your abdomen, taking slower, deeper breaths. If you make a habit of meditating, you'll find that you are generally more relaxed and can turn to this helpful practice when needed. There are a number of apps and videos that you can use to guide you in mindfulness and breathing exercises.

Sometimes just taking a break to get some fresh air can help. Get away for a long weekend, take a vacation out of town, or take a staycation in your own community. Exercise and healthy eating habits also are good stress relievers.

When you begin to tense up, breathing is one of the best strategies to calm down. #ResilienceReady

---

If you are a person of faith, prayer and reflection through scriptures and readings help to inspire your *purpose* and shift your mindset to a positive, hopeful *perspective*. Connecting with a higher power can help you build the courage and willpower you'll need to persevere.

Take a Calculated Step Forward

The next step in building up your courage is to take a calculated step forward. It's scary to step into the unknown. Turn your energy to taking one positive step. Courage does not mean stepping out unprepared, but it does mean that you take a step. You know it's going to be uncomfortable because you can't see the outcome. You tell yourself it's going to be OK and things will only get worse if you do nothing. You can't grow until you step out and do something. You can't move forward without that first step. From there, it's one step at a time. Courage happens in these most uncomfortable, vulnerable spaces.

Your calculated step forward is not the brain's amygdala reactionary response. In the heat of the moment, you often feel like you have to do something immediately. Moving your thoughts from your amygdala to the prefrontal neocortex area of your brain takes only a second, but requires intention. You want to form the habit of stopping momentarily to be more thoughtful before you react. Then you can contemplate your options to get to the outcome you want from the situation at that moment.

Everything won't go perfectly. Taking a calculated step means there is still a bit of risk. Give yourself some grace from expecting that you have to be perfect. It's easy to get stuck in "dotting every i" and "crossing every t" before you take action. However, inaction and perfection are your greatest enemies. This first calculated step will be your thrust toward the Courageous Stage and Thriving Stage of internal crisis response.

Nackia Salmon recalled the emotion that drives her forward: "I try again because the fear of what I will be if I stay in the current state is *greater* than what I ever need to muster inside to take 'the next step forward.' If I just identify the next step, I'll know if I can do it by myself or who I can call for help."

As a leader, when you demonstrate courage, along with grace, you empower others to find their own courage. Your employees need to know that they can take a calculated step without fearing retribution. Your expectations and how you respond to your employees in times of risk and uncertainty have a significant impact on whether your team will remain stuck or become courageous.

Courage can be a light of hope for yourself and encourage others.

Step 2. Roadmap Your Path Forward

Going beyond the first step takes planning and more thoughtful consideration of the situation. Your initial calculated step forward likely involves action in this direction. Where do you go from here?

Look for a few close allies early on who share your vision. They can help influence others in gaining buy-in to the vision. They also can provide insight on others' thoughts and concerns that require consideration.

An action plan removes stress and brings the team together. Your objective is to begin to look at your options, exploring and researching their potential; then you assess them, and return to align those potential options with your desired goals and outcomes in a *very* specific and intentional way.

It's ideal to use a problem-solving approach to planning, organizing, and executing your actions. Utilize the expertise within your organization in Project Management or Lean Six Sigma — disciplines in continuous process improvement — to lead this work.

Identify & Narrow Potential Options

The following steps and assessment questions will guide you in identifying potential options in response to the crisis, and narrowing the potential options to the most probable path forward (given the situation) as well as your organizational capabilities, challenges, and goals.

a) *Engage your team* — There are several ways engaging your team will enhance your plan and outcomes. Solving a problem together creates a bond with team members. They are working together through a challenge and toward a common cause and outcome. They have each other for support, especially when the challenge seems insurmountable. You also get collective energy from working together. There's greater ownership in the plan and making it work. You generate a diversity of ideas. There's a greater sense of group identity and pride in fighting for and achieving your goals.

b) *Align with the goals and outcomes you wish to accomplish* — Bring your purpose front and center. What are the most important priorities for your focus? What is the vision for the outcome you wish to achieve? How should you organize the work into sub-projects focused on specific goals and deliverables that contribute to the fulfillment of your purpose?

c) *Consider your current situation analysis* — What were the key takeaways from the assessment of your current situation? What realities are you dealing with? What is the real problem or challenge you're trying to solve? Where do you believe you are now in the lifecycle of the crisis, and how is the situation evolving?

d) *Benchmark, inside and outside of your industry* — What solutions are beginning to surface within the industry; outside of the industry? How have historical crises with similar characteristics been addressed?

e) *Explore a variety of options* — Which options are viable to move you toward fulfilling your purpose? What possible paths are options to achieving your goals? What resources will be required? What criteria should you use to evaluate each option?

f) *Consider parallel paths and contingencies* — What are the possible scenarios for how this crisis will evolve? How might that alter your plans? What are the potential risks? What contingency plans should be in place to enable you to mitigate those risks or to quickly respond as the situation evolves?

g) *Narrow to the most probable* — Which scenarios are most likely to accomplish your goals and purpose? Assess different options based on important variables such as the effort or investment required compared to the outcome each option is likely to achieve. A matrix is often useful to assess each option against different criteria, such as the effort required compared to the value of the anticipated outcome. From this analysis, you'll have a prioritization of options that are most likely to accomplish your purpose, including options to help you respond with agility as the crisis evolves. Don't get bogged down with "things that would be nice to do" but add little value to solving the current pressing problem.

Defining Your Next Steps

Now that you have prioritized options for your path forward, it's time to determine and outline the action steps to get you moving beyond your initial calculated step forward. Keep your vision uppermost in your mind to keep you focused on the most important actions.

One of the first questions you'll ask is, "What are your most important next steps to begin moving on this plan?" Be careful not to overcomplicate it. Seeing a path out of a crisis can seem ominous. Break actions into smaller, manageable steps. Establish milestones with rewards so you can celebrate your progress.

Keep your vision uppermost in your mind to keep you focused on the most important actions. #ResilienceReady

Determine how you can implement a pilot to learn quickly on a small scale and minimize your risk going forward. Your lessons learned will help you refine your plan, better identify resource requirements at scale, and avoid unnecessary costs and mistakes.

Set yourself up for success by building in accountability. Engage the team in assigning deadlines and responsibilities. Ensure expectations are clearly communicated and understood.

How do you put structure around your action items in order to be more likely to follow through?

So often, organizations forget to ensure that policies, processes, and systems are in place to support the work they ask employees to do. In a crisis situation, these may fall outside of normal operating procedures. Identify needs based on the plans with which you've decided to move forward. Check back frequently to be certain your previous solutions are still in place and not eroding. This is critical in setting up your teams for success.

Set team and individual priorities so that everyone is clear on where to direct time and resources. This will require conversations about day-to-day responsibilities that may be in conflict with the need to prioritize crisis-related tasks. This is a good time to ask, "What are we currently doing that shouldn't be done at all?"

Step 3. Take Decisive Action

Ready! Set! Go! You've established momentum by courageously taking the first calculated steps. Now keep it going by courageously continuing to act according to your plan.

Measure and track the progress toward your goals. Even small successes have a huge impact on your progress. Make sure you recognize and celebrate individual and team accomplishments.

Sometimes the best laid plans need to change, especially with the unpredictability of a crisis. Again, give yourself some grace when things don't go perfectly. Be ready to shift and change with the situation, which may require a plan adjustment.

Remain Agile

Mountain climbers must be constantly aware of the conditions around them and attempt to anticipate what's ahead. As part of their expedition preparation they plan for contingencies, so they can adapt with agility through changing conditions.

Without agility, you risk being stuck in an unfavorable and vulnerable position. The exposure leaves you open to even greater risk, with an even tougher climb ahead as a result. You risk missing opportunities that you hadn't previously explored.

Even during a crisis, you may have more control over the outcome than you may realize. Agility is a proactive tool that offers greater control.

Carmen Moreno-Rivera recalled a time when agility was critical for her team. "When I worked at UPS, I was on shift the day of the Flight 1354 crash in Birmingham, AL. We got the call and went into crisis mode — you grab the book, you call people, you activate contingency plans; there are procedures in place for that portion. I started to see the agility come out in different people. There were leaders who could be vulnerable and talk to people, serve that role. You had people who could come back and report on the facts, 'this is where we are in the process.' You had those folks who, like myself, came in as a shift leader to work with the team, 'here's what we're going to be doing tonight at work;' just understanding that people needed to focus on something and that that focus is different for everybody. So here's the work plan and let's work on that. In those days after, I felt like we saw a diverse team just jump in with 'here's what we need to do.' And we all got through it based on the team's collective action."

How can you be an agile leader?

Be Informed

Determine sources of real-time information. Be aware, listen, and consider what the information means for you. How does the situation impact your organization? Stay aware so you're not caught completely off guard. Avoid knee-jerk reactions to every new bit of information, but have a process in place for careful consideration, and recognize potential risks. Develop a small group of three or four connected individuals who will give you honest feedback on how the team is responding. You want to know what employees are not telling you directly.

Envision the Bigger Picture

Golf instructors teach you to close your eyes and visualize your shot before striking the ball — how far to hit it, how high, and where to land the ball. To remain agile, you must envision the bigger picture first. Make sure your organization's desired outcomes remain front and center considering the current environment. What has to happen right now to mitigate the crisis? What impact has the crisis had on your priorities, and across your operations? Also consider how the team's decisions and actions will impact the organization as a whole. It's easy for your attention to get diverted to less important priorities and the "noise" going on around you.

Set Incremental Goals

Agility takes a shorter-term view. What can be and needs to be accomplished in the near term? What are the more immediate priorities and opportunities? What can we do now that can benefit our employees, our customers, our community? How does that contribute to accomplishing our longer-term goals? Setting and achieving incremental milestones helps you deliver more frequent value.

Be Flexible

The best laid plans sometimes need to change. To be agile, you need a process to consider new information, and to be flexible, making adjustments as needed. Don't be married to just one way of doing things; especially your way. "There are many ways to get from point A to point B. That's OK," explained John Hackett. "The important thing is you are moving in the right direction and not going the other way." Have a core team who will connect on a regular basis to evaluate the current state of the situation and your planned response. Don't look at the need to adapt your plans as failure, but rather as a strength in that you can be responsive.

As an agile leader, you can respond to the dynamics of a changing environment in real time. #ResilienceReady

You also have to be flexible about how work gets done. A crisis brings about unexpected working conditions. For example, a flood may require you to close your plant or offices and have employees work from home. Employees may be asked to work on different committees and may have to take on extra work. Invite input from the team on how they can work most effectively, both independently and collaboratively.

Remember, as an agile leader you can respond to the dynamics of a changing environment in real time.

Action Empowers

There will be times when taking action feels heavy and overwhelming. But taking action opens the space where energy, hope, confidence, and willpower can strengthen, both individually and as a team. Even if steps aren't all perfectly mapped out and the path forward seems daunting, small steps will add up to progress. Encourage and recognize action among your team. Don't expect perfection, but coach them toward doing a reasonable due diligence, rather than getting caught up in analysis paralysis. Create an environment of calculated and informed risk taking, ensuring your response does not reprimand when mistakes or failure occur. Use these as coaching opportunities to review what went well and lessons learned from the experience.

Consider This

Rate yourself and your team on a scale of 1 (disagree) to 5 (agree) on the following statements about how you tend to make and take action on decisions.

Myself

______ I can quickly analyze available information and make a decision I'm pretty confident in.

______ Once I make a decision, I'm ready to take action.

______ I am flexible in making adjustments to a plan if needed.

My Team

______ My team can quickly analyze available information and make a decision we're pretty confident in.

______ Once we make a decision, we're ready to take action.

______ We are flexible in making adjustments to a plan if needed.

For the questions you rated 3 or below, what tends to get in the way?

____

It's Time to Lead with Perseverance!

Giving up leaves you and your team deflated and powerless. With clarity around a meaningful *purpose*, *perseverance* becomes "worth it." With a *perspective* that reminds you that "we can do this" and that "excellence, rather than perfection" is the goal, *perseverance* becomes easier and getting through the crisis seems doable.

You can look back and feel good about being able to say "I gave it my best shot."

Remember:

→ Perseverance is not only a state of mind, but it's also how you can physically reverse the inertia that can trap you when you lack control.

→ Perseverance is nonexistent without Perspective and Purpose, Resilience Principles 1 and 2, which give you the psychological foundation that you can overcome and that it's worth the struggle. These principles provide inspiration to take on the tough times ahead.

→ When your team works together to persevere through the struggles, team morale grows, productivity increases, and operating results improve.

→ Perseverance requires:

- *Step 1. Setting the stage for the environment*
- *Step 2. Roadmapping your path forward by preparing and planning*
- *Step 3. Taking decisive action*

Resilience Ready Today

Rapid Start Activity

PRINCIPLE 3. PERSEVERANCE

Goal: Discover the psychological, emotional, and physical strength to push through the adversity regardless of what you're facing.

Following are the most immediate reflections or actions that will get you on the path toward becoming a Resilience Ready Leader. Engage your team to inspire team resilience.

Step 1. Set the Environment

Courage

Reflections

Face Your FEAR

1. What were your biggest fears or concerns during the most recent crisis? How did they impact you?

Reframe Your Stress

1. How did those fears or concerns create stress for you?
2. What is most helpful for you in relieving stress?

Take Action

Reframe Your Stress

1. Take a stress assessment to get an objective idea of your level of stress and possible contributors.
2. Be observant of your team's experience. Be intentional in addressing contributors and providing support toward reducing stress.

Inspiring Team Resilience Discussion Questions

Take Action

- Download the "Inspiring Team Resilience — Perseverance Discussion Questions" and schedule time to have discussions with your team. Visit https://ResilienceReady.today.

Resources

You may wish to use the accompanying *Resilience Reader Leader's Guide* workbook to complete these exercises. Additional resources also are available at https://ResilienceReady.today.

If you need support with assessments and in taking action, contact me at vivian@vivianblade.com

Chapter 8

Partnership

RESILIENCE READY PRINCIPLE 4

"Coming together is a beginning. Keeping together is progress. Working together is success." — Henry Ford

"I think the best of us comes when we are working together collectively." — Martin Luther King, Jr. III

"Our regular supplier was trying to rebuild from the fire while we were busy working with backup suppliers to qualify them and ramp up production," Tim described. "Our teams were working extra hours, taking on responsibilities outside of our day-to-day jobs. You could tell that employees were still quite stressed. We were asking a lot of people, and they were stepping up to the plate, sacrificing a lot of their own personal time to pitch in. Kayla and I often would check in and have conversations with employees about how to manage the workload, and concerns about the fallout from this disruption. We tried to listen and just let them know that they were heard. That seemed to help more than anything.

"Several new work teams were established based on recommendations from the crisis response teams. We needed employees from different functional areas and with specific expertise in some cases. As leaders selected talent for these teams, we wanted to be conscientious that they didn't hurriedly just pick their same 'go-to' people. Kayla made it a point to collaborate closely with Human Resources to carefully consider a diverse array of potential employees for these teams. We advocated for broad diversity and planned some initial 'get to know you' lunches and happy hours to begin team building.

"We wanted to make sure everyone felt welcome, were comfortable contributing, and that we established positive, constructive working relationships, because the pace would be fast, with a lot of attention focused on these teams. We also spent a lot of time with these teams getting them to high performing, putting more intention around helping them work out team norms, roles, and responsibilities, and work processes. Partnerships between team members, across teams, across departments, with suppliers and other outside groups would be critical if we were going to work our way out of this dilemma."

Why Partnership Is Important to Achieving Resilience

Partnership is about the connection you form with others who are sharing a common experience and working together toward a common goal. True partnership is giving up titles and ego, and jumping in to see where you can help, to do what needs to be done. There's nothing like a crisis to bring people together. "We're all in this together" sounds somewhat cliché. But when everyone is vulnerable to the unknown, you find that you have more in common with others than you thought, and that you need each other even in order to simply survive.

True partnership is giving up titles and ego, and jumping in to see where you can help, to do what needs to be done. #ResilienceReady

Nackia Salmon shared how partnership has been important to her: "When I am at the end of myself, I raise my hands and ask for help. I have learned that I am as strong as my relationships. At my very greatest storms, there was someone there to help. Sometimes not always who you expect. The universe has a way to deliver if you pay attention."

My daughter and I walked outside our front door one morning and noticed a line of at least 100 ants intently traveling from the dirt on one side of the sidewalk to the other. They traveled in a straight line in either direction, coming and going. We looked closer to see what this trail of ants was up to. As they got over to one side of the sidewalk, they were picking up a small white speck of what we assume was food and traveling back to the other side of the sidewalk into the dirt. They had a system. They were all in sync, following each other at the same speed so that the lines flowed seamlessly in either direction. We came back to the sidewalk about fifteen minutes later, and there was a much smaller group of ants still on the trail. When we returned about an hour later, they were gone. They had finished their work. Each ant knew what needed to be done and was playing its part. They were committed to the outcome, working in partnership with each other, supporting one another, each accountable in their role toward accomplishing their goal.

Like ants, people have a basic need for socialization and community. Psychologist Abraham Maslow found in his research that you must meet your need for belonging and interpersonal relationships before you can realize needs for esteem and self-actualization. The communities you belong to personally and professionally play a significant role in your existence and survival. Resilience improves when you have a support system of people both encouraging you and pitching in.

Engagement research demonstrates the importance of partnership in the workplace and having leaders who can foster a culture of partnership. Results from Gallup's engagement research finds that in addition to meaningful work, relationships at work, especially with a manager who is invested in coaching employees to the next level, is a key driver of engagement. Gallup reports from their "Q12 Employee Engagement Survey" that "the manager or team leader alone accounts for 70% of the variance in team engagement." Of the twelve drivers of engagement from Gallup's annual study, all include some element of partnership, from a demonstration of care, connecting employees to purpose, to fostering genuine, caring relationships, to investing in their growth.

How a Crisis Impacts Partnership

The strain of a crisis tests those working relationships that are so critical to partnership. There's greater pressure coming from all directions, and the work environment is often tense. This can either strengthen or dilute partnership. How this plays out will be affected by the organizational culture as it relates to the strength of its values, purpose, engagement practices, and team dynamics.

People will partner when they have a purpose that is important to them to rally around. When they feel a personal connection to a genuine purpose and feel that their work is important in making a difference, they will enroll with passion and commitment. Working toward that purpose with others, knowing that the collective effort can make a bigger impact than individually, inspires their engagement.

People will partner when they have a purpose that is important to them to rally around. #ResilienceReady

During the time of the Civil Rights Movement, the United States was in crisis because of the human injustice toward people of color. This movement ultimately engaged people of different races in fighting for justice for all people. As the movement grew, more and more people were joining together toward this common purpose. Their purpose was significant, their perspective hopeful, and their perseverance unwavering. People in the movement were willing to give up their lives, and many did, for the greater good. Dr. Martin Luther King, Jr. and other leaders of the movement were able to bring many different constituents together, though motives may have varied, in partnership to make change happen with the signing of the Civil Rights Act of 1964, achieving a significant step toward cultural change across this country.

Power Threatens Partnership

Racial inequality has created extreme division within the United States since the inception of slavery. The threat of losing power many times throughout our country's history has allowed the injustice to continue for centuries, even into the 21st century. When power is threatened, partnership is diluted. The signing of the Emancipation Proclamation by President Abraham Lincoln in 1863 and the Civil Rights Movement of the 1950s and 1960s, two significant events in our history, threatened this country's system of power and privilege. The threat of this change caused those in power to resist the movement with greater injustice through physical violence and legislative indignation.

Rather than partnering together to seek innovative solutions for a more just and fair society that could benefit all, those against equality partnered together to continue their fight, while others turned their heads or have been blind to injustices that still exist. This continuation of a lack of partnership led to the resurgence of protests against racial injustice with the Black Lives Matter movement. The exposure of other forms of social injustice have produced the #MeToo movement and protests against injustices in the U.S. immigration system.

Because the dynamics of a crisis can create division and inequities, you must be even more intentional about bringing people and teams together for support, and to work together toward an improved future state.

A crisis can produce extreme vulnerability due to uncertainty and lack of control. Your natural instinct is to do what you can to protect yourself, both emotionally and physically. In the face of challenge you can feel everyone watching; you believe you have to come across as strong. Even though you put a facade on the outside, inside you feel "less than" and insecure. This can lead to a strong pushback to change. Another response may be emotional, psychological, and physical isolation, given the strength of your insecurities.

Consequences When Partnership Is Broken

A lack of partnership destroys great societies, communities, organizations, and teams. Early in my career I observed fallout from the leadership style of our Vice President of Marketing. A lot of people were fearful of him because of his commanding approach and often demeaning interactions. The department was highly competitive rather than collaborative.

A lack of partnership destroys great societies, communities, organizations, and teams. #ResilienceReady

People were protective, not sharing information or resources so they could use them to their personal advantage. Heated discussions were commonplace. There were a handful of "favored" employees whom others talked about unfavorably. The Director of Marketing and other highly talented individuals left the company. That situation left a definite impression on me. Thankfully, instances of this type of leader and work environment were rare in my career.

Some of the consequences resulting from poor partnership can be witnessed in the following ways:

- Trust is challenged — Early on in a crisis, there's a lack of reliable information. As a result, rumors spiral based on information that emerges from sources that appear credible. Employees are afraid that leaders are not being transparent and they are not getting the truth. Employees may not trust leaders to make the decisions that are in their best interest.
- Isolation — Isolation can be brought on when a crisis requires physical separation. Team dynamics are affected when teams are not together. You have to reengineer how work gets done. I often hear from clients who have employees working remotely of the struggles to ensure everyone is connected. "Out of sight, out of mind" is a risk. It's important to find new ways of staying connected with each other and be intentional about making those new practices the norm.
- No one cares — A high-pressure work environment is often demanding and competitive. In sink-or-swim mode, there's a strong focus on figuring out how to get through the crisis. Leaders are not as attentive to the needs or experiences of individual employees, expecting them to do whatever it takes to get work done. Employees can feel like neither their manager nor employer cares about their well-being.
- Individualism — The competitive nature of the work environment can lead to individualism, where teams are not working together toward a common purpose. Employees are trying to get their own work done and don't have the bandwidth to help their colleagues. Teams are not communicating effectively.
- Disconnected priorities — Poor partnership also comes from a lack of clear direction and expectations. Employees are

working on different priorities. There's a lack of coordinated effort, which impacts employee and team performance. Engagement wanes.

- Employee turnover increases — When employees don't feel supported or work in an unhealthy team culture, they become frustrated and disengaged in the workplace. Higher rates of employee disengagement result in higher rates of employee turnover.
- Internal focus vs. external focus — When partnership is weak, the culture is focused on internal problems and discourse. You think you know what the customer needs and wants. You're focused on what is most convenient and cost effective for you rather than what is most important to customers. You fail to invest resources back into the communities where you operate, and fail to make them better places to work and live.

Advantages When Partnership Is Strong

The deadline for the implementation of regulatory requirements was approaching for a regional utility company. They were concerned that they may not have been ready to make the significant investments required to implement the regulations. Missing the windows for the implementation timetable would result in steep fines. My client Jan had recently been promoted to the role of compliance manager and needed to ensure that various department leaders, and their teams, were on board. These functional leaders were owners of the projects and budgets needed to meet the new regulatory requirements.

Once she got her arms around the status, Jan's next move was building partnerships across the departments involved, starting with the leaders. She met with each department leader and their teams to understand any concerns and roadblocks. The departments regrouped around the purpose of implementing the changes, and the anticipated impact on the customer experience. They worked through competing priorities and roadblocks to determine how they could best partner to get the

Partnership is integrated in the culture and demonstrated in everything you do. #ResilienceReady

implementation done on schedule. Instead of working in silos, they came together as "one team" to meet the requirements before the deadline.

Organizations whose leaders are intentional about building partnership emerge stronger through a crisis. They experience the following benefits:

- Increased buy-in — Employees and customers are bought in to the purpose because they were included and involved in its defining.
- Partnership is genuinely demonstrated, not just talked about — Leaders don't just give lip service to what they claim are important values; partnership is integrated in the culture and demonstrated in everything they do. They realize that strong partnerships are a significant source of progress in the Thriving Stage. Employees work day-to-day in partnership with each other and with customers. The culture is such that teams and individuals are effectively collaborating and communicating, rather than competing with one another. Individuals and teams are collaborating and communicating effectively. Through teams, organizations get more value-add work done.
- A greater sense of belonging strengthens engagement and commitment — The "Trust Index Employee Survey" results from the 2019 "World's Best Workplaces," finds that among employees who work for these "Best Workplaces" organizations, collaboration, productivity, and retention are all higher. Employees are more willing to give 110%. Well over 90% of employees who work for companies such as Workday, Adobe, and McDonalds report that partnership begins to build as soon as they join the company. They are welcomed and treated fairly. As a result, they are proud of the company.
- Customers are more committed and loyal — Partnership can be measured by the customer experience. A consumer benchmark study by Qualtrics XM Institute of 10,000 U.S. consumers across 20 industries found that a customer's experience influences their likelihood to purchase more, to recommend, forgive, and trust a company, as well as to try a new product or service from that company. The data showed

that "94% of consumers who give a company a 'very good' CX (customer service) rating are 'very likely' to purchase more products or services from that company in the future, while only 18% of those who gave a company a 'very poor' CX rating say the same." The study also found that "90% of consumers who give a company a 'very good' CX rating are 'very likely' to trust a company to take care of their needs, while only 15% of those who gave a company a 'very poor' CX rating say the same."

- Organizations partner in helping employees develop and grow — According to Gallup engagement research, organizations that have seen steady increases in employee engagement "have focused on creating high-development cultures, where people can see their impact on the organization and its customers through their work. They have opportunities to develop their strengths and purpose into a career."

Consider This

What benefits have you realized when strong partnership exists within your team?

Steps to Becoming Resilience Ready

Servant Leadership Through Partnership

Lead with "what can I do for you" and "together, how can we get through this crisis?" #ResilienceReady

Partnership is not about "what can you do for me?" Lead with "what can I do for you" and "together, how can we get through this crisis?" Your intention must be to partner for mutual benefit. That is the spirit of a servant leader.

Tonya Jackson describes how partnership played a role in her team's culture: "I was taken by the comments from a gentleman who joined our team from another company. He expressed how he could feel that everybody was working together, not just within supply chain, but across the organization. I like to say that supply chain means a chain, and we're no stronger than each link. We are connected. If a customer doesn't get a product, it is not because of this group or that group. We don't place blame. My metric is 'was the customer served?' If one group has to do something unusual in order for another piece of the organization to succeed, we just make those tradeoffs. Everyone's voice in the decision-making process is heard and we will disagree during that discussion. But at the end of the discussion, our team culture is such that everybody can align to the decision and can move forward together."

A resilient leader is an "others first" focused leader, a selfless leader, a servant leader. A resilient leader's priority is others over self. Servant leadership is concerned with striving to make a human connection with people built on a foundation of respect and a genuine concern for the others' well-being. You can't build partnership without this spirit.

A servant leader who builds partnership invests in building and maintaining positive, healthy relationships on an ongoing basis. You need to have built some relationship capital by the time you need to call on someone for help during a crisis. Don't wait to reach out to people only when you need something.

The other four Resilience Ready Principles — Perspective, Purpose, Perseverance, and Praise — are foundational to Partnership. What role do they play?

- Perspective — A positive, hopeful perspective supports the belief in the ability to get through the crisis, and sets the tone for the work together as a team.
- Purpose — People need a strong purpose or cause to rally around and inspire them. You have to affect people emotionally and intellectually to engage their commitment to move through the turbulence of the crisis and get to the vision for your post-crisis state.
- Perseverance provides the collective will and momentum to make it over the bridge to the future.
- Praise — Our human spirit needs inspiration to keep going, especially in a crisis. Recognition for the effort, the hurdles overcome, and the accomplishments says, "I see you," and opens the door for mutual partnership to occur.

Partnership has the potential to produce powerful outcomes when there's synergy among the team. Elizabeth Hill, M.A., Early Childhood Development and an expert on the subject, recalled hearing a report on National Public Radio that described how a new pharmaceutical drug had been developed through the combination of two existing drugs. The synergy of the two drugs combined created a pharmaceutical effect that was not just duplicative, but novel and exponential. "The synergy produced by working together in partnership has a similar creative and exponential effect," Elizabeth describes.

Synergy within teams and organizations creates the opportunity for innovation, because the multiplier is the effect of many minds, talents, skills, etc., working toward the same goal. "The synergistic effect derives, in part, implicitly from the inherent value in each partner, from that value being recognized and acknowledged by the other partners, and from the opportunity or pathway for each partner's value, capacity, and potential contribution to be expressed," Elizabeth further explains.

Steps to Build & Strengthen Partnership

Three servant leadership practices are instrumental for resilient leaders in building partnership:

Step 1. Practice ***empathy***
Step 2. Build ***diverse, equitable, and inclusive partnerships***
Step 3. SCALE your ***influence***

Step 1. Practice Empathy

Have you walked a mile in someone else's shoes? Probably not literally, but you can do this figuratively. Empathy is important to building partnership because, when demonstrated, you connect to others where they are. Showing empathy says to the other person, "I can appreciate what you're going through." You may not have had an identical experience. You may not agree with their concern. Neither is required. You also are not required to take on their emotion — sadness, hurt, anger. You imagine what it would be like to be in their shoes and make space for them to work through their emotion. People just want to be heard respectfully. Our brains and hearts have to work through the situations that confront us. You may not agree that they should have that emotion or concern. This is not for you to judge.

Empathy is important to building partnership because, when demonstrated, you connect to others where they are. #ResilienceReady

---

How to Practice Empathy

Listen & Acknowledge

What is required to demonstrate empathy is that you recognize the other person is going through a challenging time and acknowledge that they are in this space. Your job is to listen without trying to minimize their concern or fix the situation with your solutions. You can respond with a statement that acknowledges they have been heard, such as "That sounds really difficult. I hear your concern. I can appreciate how that must make you feel." It is not until this step happens that one is able to move past the emotion and roadblock. The act of acknowledgement makes internal space for the person to begin to work toward resolution. This is a good time to move the discussion forward with a coaching approach, which uses questions to guide them to find solutions within themselves.

Change is difficult, especially when it is unexpected and of significant impact. Uncertainty creates anxiety and concern. Even though you may believe fears are unfounded, for those who have them, they are very real. Put yourself in the other person's shoes to see the situation from their perspective. Remember a time when you were in a similar situation or emotional state. What were you going through, and how did it feel to have someone empathetic who listened to you?

Proactively Check-In

Make it a habit to proactively reach out and check-in with each individual on your team. Andrea Towns shared a practice that she uses to check-in with her team: "I have virtual teatime with individual team members. We actually block time out on the calendar. We don't talk about work. We just check-in with each other." You may recognize that someone is stressed and has a lot on their mind. Invite and make time for conversation. Instead of talking, listen empathetically with genuine concern. Be present in the moment so that you can really hear what is being said and sense what is coming across to you in words, emotions, and nonverbal cues. Respond in a way that lets people know they are heard, without trying to have all the answers.

Focus on What's Important

Team members may be worried about things that are invisible to you, such as feeding their families, caring for children, tending to elderly parents, or dealing with illness, all while trying to manage their workload. Focus on what's most important, and be considerate with deadlines, given all the balls people are trying to juggle. Don't get wrapped around insignificant rules or protocols (such as how many hours someone worked today). Focus on outcomes and results. Your employees will go above and beyond when it's really needed if you do the same when they really need you.

Make Space for Processing & Sharing

Make space for employees to talk with each other to process and realize others share similar concerns. This creates a bond where employees are more likely to support each other and work together to find solutions to get through the challenges.

At work, people feel like they can't be vulnerable by sharing emotions or concerns. The expectation is to always "have it together," or to act like you do anyway. Create an environment where people care about each other's well-being. Support resources can often be accessed through the company's employee assistance program (EAP). Make sure you are aware of the available resources and contact information to pass on to employees.

Create an environment where people care about each other each other's well-being. #ResilienceReady

---

Step 2. Build Diverse, Equitable, & Inclusive Partnerships

The Society for Human Resource Management explains that "Diversity refers to the similarities and differences among individuals, accounting for all aspects of their personality and individual identity." Race, gender, and sexual orientation are often among the first characteristics people think of related to diversity. There is a vast array of characteristics that intersect to make us who we are — economic, gender identity, life experiences, culture, disability, education, and family status, to name a few.

"Equity in the workplace refers to fair treatment in access, opportunity, and advancement for all individuals. Work in this area includes identifying and working to eliminate barriers to fair treatment for disadvantaged groups, from the team level through systemic changes in organizations and industries," describes the Society for Human

Resource Management (SHRM). Organizational culture, through your policies, practices, priorities, values, and behaviors, influence the degree to which equity is realized.

"Inclusion describes the extent to which each person in an organization feels welcomed, respected, supported, and valued as a team member," as defined by the SHRM. While leaders say that inclusion is important, the experience of employees often does not match what leaders believe is happening. In a study among leaders and employers, Accenture found that "two thirds of leaders (68 percent) feel they create empowering environments — in which employees can be themselves, raise concerns, and innovate without fear of failure — but just one third (36 percent) of employees agree." Clearly there is work to be done.

Diversity, Equity, & Inclusion Make Business & Moral Sense

Forming diverse, equitable, and inclusive workplaces are critical to building partnership. It is evident in business results. Studies on inclusion by McKinsey & Company since 2014 have shown a greater likelihood that businesses with more diverse representation outperform companies with lower percentages of diversity among their ranks. Financial outperformance was up to 25% more likely by gender diversity and up to 36% more likely by racial diversity.

Resilience is not possible if organizations do not value or build diversity, equity, and inclusion into the fabric of their culture and infrastructure. #ResilienceReady

Diversity, equity, and inclusion are essential to strengthen business outcomes and partnerships. As a servant leader, these are imperative because you care.

Resilience is not possible if organizations do not value or build diversity, equity, and inclusion into the fabric of their culture and infrastructure.

Following are specific steps you can take to begin shifting the culture of your organization.

How to Build Diverse, Equitable, and Inclusive Partnerships

Expand Your Circle

Take a minute to think about the people or groups who are your usual "go to's" for information or help, and who are within your more informal circle of acquaintances and allies. Are they more like you or are they diverse? Are you intentional about reaching out to those who bring diversity of thought, opinion, work experiences, life experiences, race, gender, or sexual orientation? Your human nature is to be most comfortable with people who are most like you.

In order to be inclusive of a wide spectrum of individuals, you must be intentional in reaching out to engage people who are *not* most like you. Be aware that your biases, whether conscious or unconscious, are getting in your way of engaging others. Biases are ingrained in societal culture and norms. As we learn these biases, we accept them as normal or "just the way things are." Which of your personal biases are keeping you from creating an inclusive work environment?

Create Equal Opportunities to Contribute

Because everything moves so fast, it often feels like there's not enough time to plan, let alone solicit input from the team. Also, it's harder to engage everyone when the team is dispersed. Certainly there will be some urgent decisions that you'll need to make. Those should be few. Engage the team in setting direction, priorities, and action plans. People want to be involved and to feel a sense of ownership in work-related decisions.

Be intentional and ensure everyone has an equal opportunity to contribute. It's easy to go to the same few people with whom you are most comfortable. The result will be alienated, disengaged team members. By failing to gather diverse ideas you risk less than optimal business results and possible attrition of highly capable talent.

Go Beyond the Obvious

Realize that different groups of people will experience a crisis differently. Though the shared challenge tends to bring people together, people may be suffering in different ways. Societal racial inequities in areas such as education, jobs, economics, and housing meant that African Americans experienced the greatest exposure and impact in crises such as Hurricane Katrina, the Great Recession, and the COVID-19 pandemic. Consider factors that may not be evident when attempting to understand a person's needs and response during a crisis.

Realize that the ways different groups of people experience a crisis are different. #ResilienceReady

Carmen Moreno-Rivera, Chief of Performance Improvement with the Louisville, KY Metro Government, has first-hand understanding of the inequities experienced by diverse populations. "Those inequities are built on a system of historical injustice in our laws, regulations, and policies that will take time to change. Being in this leadership position, I have a responsibility to raise awareness of the inequities, and to do what I can to bring about change." She encourages leaders to be mindful that systemic inequities exist, and to make space for people of all races within their organizations to process and share their experiences. Change cannot take place without the awareness of its necessity.

Invest in Building Inclusive Partnerships

You will have to build partnerships with a variety of stakeholders, all with different needs, so your approach with each will vary. Consider external stakeholders such as customers, vendors, regulatory agencies, and communities where your employees and operations are based, in addition to team members, colleagues, various groups, departments, and individuals across your organization. Each may play an important role in getting through the crisis.

Building One-on-one Partnership

Change in creating organizational inclusion begins at an individual level. Building one-on-one partnership begins with investing in a one-on-one relationship. Each person on your team is different and has unique needs. Schedule intentional time to meet with each of them. Understand each person's story and how they are experiencing the crisis. What does each person have to contribute? What are their concerns? What support would be beneficial to get through the crisis? What do they need in order to feel included? Knowledge grows understanding, and understanding grows trust and respect. Invite individuals to contribute their ideas and talents.

> ***Change in creating organizational inclusion begins at an individual level. #ResilienceReady***

Professionals often share the feelings of exclusion when working in an environment where cliques are prevalent; this may stem from biases, organizational hierarchy, or job type. For example, in healthcare, different roles are represented by wearing different color scrubs, making it easy to tell who belongs to which work group. Each group may have lunch or take breaks only with people in similar roles.

Gallup's research findings on the twelve drivers of employee engagement are an excellent reference for factors that matter to employees. Build partnership around these areas. Here are a few ideas:

- Demonstrate that you genuinely respect and care about each individual.
- Understand their interests and skills so that their work is in alignment.
- Invest in their development based on interests and skill gaps that can lead toward career advancement.

A person's willingness to partner and to commit will be heavily influenced by the inclusiveness of the work environment and trusted relationships with leaders, direct supervisors, and team members.

Building Team Partnership

How you work as a team may adjust during a crisis. We saw this most explicitly during the COVID-19 crisis. With social distancing requirements, organizations were forced to go to remote work arrangements to follow Center for Disease Control guidelines in order to keep employees safe. New teams form during crises to address various areas of crisis response. These teams should be cross-functional and inclusive, representative of diverse groups across the organization. Make sure the culture and norms of your team are inclusive, ensuring all voices have an opportunity for a seat at the table and to be heard.

Be aware that there is a process teams go through to get to a point of partnership, and to be highly productive working together. In the mid-1960s, Bruce Tuckman, psychologist and researcher in team dynamics, introduced the four stages of team development (with the fifth stage added in 1977) that provide a framework still relevant for identifying and understanding behavioral patterns among teams. The five stages are summarized below:

Forming — The structure around teams begins to form, outlining the team's mission, defining the organization structure, organizing work teams, and defining roles, both formally and informally.

Storming — Teams are figuring out their informal centers of power and influence. Interpersonal conflict may escalate. Productivity is below its potential capacity.

Norming — Group cohesion begins to develop. Teams begin to determine how work will get done, identifying systems and processes, and clarifying roles and responsibilities. Clarity takes shape around team cultural and operating norms. Trust begins to build.

Performing — Teams are in their "flow." They work productively together, directing energy to achieve team and organizational goals.

Adjourning — The team's dissolution ensues, whether planned or unplanned, and formalizes the closure of their work together.

Team culture and the foundation for partnership form in the earliest stages of team development. Even as a team is forming, is it inclusive? During Storming and Norming stages, working relationships, trust, and the way work gets done are determined.

The process in moving through the stages is not necessarily linear. When new members come on board, you revisit the early stages. The new team member must be integrated into the existing team. Even though they were previously functioning well, during a crisis teams may revert to earlier stages of development due to factors such as the shift of work arrangements and priorities, and team organization.

In order to become a high-functioning team, the leader must facilitate the group through the stages of development. In addition to the needs of the team, don't lose sight of the needs of each individual team member. Be attentive to team dynamics as you move through each stage, and work to ensure the team is operating in an inclusive and effective manner.

You can't wait until you are in crisis to cultivate team culture and expect to be high-functioning. #ResilienceReady

Without a diverse, inclusive team, you'll have a narrow perspective of the situation and come up with a narrow range of solutions. Build an inclusive, intersectional team that is representative of a wide range of characteristics beyond ethnicity, gender, and culture, to include factors such as generational groups, expertise, life and professional experiences, and perspectives. The power of resiliency lies in bringing the diversity together in partnership. Ensure that your organization's policies and practices are free of bias. Commit to removing your own personal biases and discomfort in hiring and engaging diverse team members.

You can't wait until you are in crisis to cultivate team culture and expect to be high-functioning. That's too late. Working through these stages and building working relationships take time. When a crisis hits, the team will either naturally follow their norms or fall into chaos if norms and performing-related habits have not already been developed.

Building External Partnerships

Customer Partnerships

Customers may need you differently during and following a crisis. They're also trying to figure out how to get through the crisis and who can help them.

Set up time to visit with customers to understand how they are doing and what they need. They may be unable to clearly define what they need; this is an area where you may be of help. Engage your team in finding ways to go the extra mile helping customers solve their challenges. Identify resources you can suggest or make available.

Supplier Partnerships

If suppliers are not doing well during a crisis, that has a direct impact on you. You are unable to meet customer needs. Be proactive in reaching out to get a feel for how the crisis has affected their business. Sharing insight on how your needs may change will help them plan for necessary adjustments and new opportunities. Identify ways you can support your suppliers while times are tough, especially smaller businesses who may not have the capital or human resources to weather the crisis. This type of partnership is mutually beneficial. Your suppliers will bend over backward to help you in a pinch because of your investment in the relationship.

Community Partnerships

Communities have to mobilize all resources to get through a crisis, and people want to make a difference in their communities. Engage your team in finding ways to give back, and give them the time to do so.

Your *purpose* includes being a good community partner, ensuring that your industry and where you operate get support to make it through a crisis. Align your offerings with your core capabilities, but be agile enough to respond to the unique needs of the moment. For example, utility companies send crews of workers to hard hit areas during hurricanes and other natural disasters to restore one of the most important resources in rebuilding communities.

Community partnership also means being willing to take a stand against injustice. Societal injustice toward minority groups continues to exist, though many pretend it is not there and sweep it under the rug. Inequality is pervasive in all realms of society, from economic, political, and social, to educational, religious, and financial. Federal, state, and local governments are seeking corporate and non-profit partners to help improve the well-being of their communities.

Internal and External Focus Required

Change starts at home. You first have to look inwardly at your organization to ensure your culture, policies, practices, and standards are diverse, equitable, and inclusive. Internally, you're looking in areas such as hiring, development, promotions, compensation, and how people are treated. Externally, you have to consider the experience of your customers and partners — is everyone treated equitably with dignity and respect?

Consider This

Community Partnership — Resilient Louisville

Carmen Moreno-Rivera, Chief of Performance Improvement with the Louisville Metro Government, pointed out that resilience is a strategic focus in the public sector. The City of Louisville's Office of Performance Improvement and the Office of Resilience and Community Services are spearheading the effort and provide this information on their website https://louisvilleky.gov/resilience.

The City of Louisville, Kentucky was selected by the Rockefeller Foundation to join the network of 100 Resilient Cities (100RC). The Resilient Louisville Strategy, developed through a collaborative community effort, serves as a roadmap to address the city's most pressing and interconnected resilience challenges. The plan and actions focus around a central theme depicted through Louisville's Resilience equation: *Resilience equals Equity plus Compassion plus Trust* (R=E+C+T).

Resilient Louisville is organized around four visions, 10 goals, and 46 action steps.

4 Visions

1. LEARN — Embrace lifelong learning
2. LIVE — Ensure a safe + healthy city
3. ENGAGE — Build a vibrant economy + place
4. THRIVE — Maximize innovation + civic engagement

Broad community participation across the metropolitan area is paramount to the call to action around this work. A Louisville Metro cross-functional team, led by the Office of Performance Improvement, heads this community partnership work.

Source: Louisville Resilience Strategy press release

To connect to more information on this initiative, visit https://ResilienceReady.today.

Step 3. SCALE Your Influence

Influence integrates several of the leadership principles covered in this book. At work and in your personal life, resilient influence takes time and requires an investment in your intention to build a reputation worthy of trust, and to build connections at a personal level.

Influence is more about how you live than what you do. #ResilienceReady

Resilient leaders use influence to build partnership with others, not to power over them. A crisis often brings about rapid change. There will be times when urgent situations require quick decisions with limited input from the team. You'll need to generate buy-in. You may need to move people to action in a given direction. Those affected have to trust that you are making the best call for their well-being.

Influence is more about how you live than what you do. Resilient influence in a way that builds partnership is not persuasion or dictating. It manifests from your actions and the experiences others have with you over time.

When I ran customer experience for GE's Consumer & Industrial Division, our goal was to use the voice of the customer to transform the experiences customers had with our products and services. Even though we regularly ran customer research in product design and to measure customer satisfaction, we needed to think about the customer in a different way. In some cases we needed to adjust our product development protocols and reconsider product development programs that were already in process. Service levels were not meeting expectations in some areas, thus requiring process changes.

My team couldn't come in with the customer research data alone to convince or dictate to the general managers that changes had to be made. Our approach was to share the information and do a lot of listening to understand their processes, concerns, and ideas. From our prior roles, my team was experienced in the intricacies of how product development, supply chains, and our services organizations worked. My team had built prior working relationships with people across the business units that also gave us credibility and resources we could go to when we had a question or needed help.

When a product quality or availability issue occurred, creating an urgent crisis situation, we were pulled in as partners to help ensure the customer experience was well thought out, carefully planned, and properly executed. We were able to SCALE our influence through the benefits of long-term partnerships.

To influence is a privilege. To be an influencer is a responsibility. #ResilienceReady

The following five principles provide a roadmap to SCALE your influence in a way that builds partnership.

- *Social Capital* — Social Capital is the dividends from the consistent investments you make in growing mutual, selfless relationships built on a foundation of empathy, genuine concern, trust, and respect. The credibility you've earned from this intentional relationship building pays off when you need buy-in, assistance, or support.
- *Courage* — Courage is overcoming your fear by facing uncertainty and having the guts to take that step forward, even though the road ahead is full of more questions than answers. Courage also is reaching out to build partnership by engaging an inclusive community with others you don't yet know or understand.
- *Authenticity* — You are self-aware, astutely conscientious, and consistent in your character, intentions, and interactions with others. You are the same person no matter what is required of you or who you are around. You may be agile, shifting your behaviors as called for in different situations, but they are consistently fundamental to who you are. Others are willing to build partnerships with you because they know you are genuine.
- *Lean-In with Passion* — You are invested in a meaningful purpose that inspires you to give your best effort. You genuinely care about the cause and the outcome, and are deeply invested because of the emotional connection to a cause, from a personal experience or because you feel that your work is fulfilling purpose in your life.

- *Engage a diverse & inclusive community* — Expand your circle inclusive of different cultures, opinions, experiences, and expertise that each contribute to a vibrant community. You generate engagement around a common interest or passion by inviting and welcoming the intersectional diversity from which others can contribute.

Real influence does not come from positional power. Real influence is earned. To influence is a privilege. To be an influencer is a responsibility.

It's Time to Lead with Partnership!

When I think of partnership, I am reminded of these familiar phrases: "Together we stand, divided we fall," and "A chain is only as strong as its weakest link." Resilient leaders build partnerships that make each other individually strong and collectively even stronger.

You can't do it alone. Resilience is impossible without strong partnerships.

Remember:

- → Partnership is about the connection you form with others who share a common experience and work together toward a common goal.
- → People will partner when they have an important purpose to rally around. When they feel a personal connection to a genuine purpose and feel that their work is important in making a difference, they will enroll with passion and commitment.
- → There are three servant leadership practices that are instrumental for resilient leaders in building partnership:
    - Practice empathy
    - Build diverse, equitable, and inclusive partnerships
    - SCALE your influence.
- → Empathy is demonstrated in acknowledging that others are going through a challenging time. Your job is to genuinely listen without trying to minimize their concern or fix the situation with your solutions.
- → "Inclusion describes the extent to which each person in an organization feels welcomed, respected, supported, and valued as a team member," as defined by the Society for Human Resource Management. Be intentional about reaching out to engage people who are *not* most like you.
- → When a crisis hits, the team will either naturally follow their norms or fall into chaos if norms and performing-related habits have not been developed.
- → Resilient leaders use influence to build partnership with others, not to power over them. Influence is more about *how* you live than *what* you do.

Resilience Ready Today

Rapid Start Activity

PRINCIPLE 4. PARTNERSHIP

Goal: Forming connections through experiences you have with others, and building on the strength of those relationships, working together to achieve a common goal.

Following are the most immediate reflections or actions that will get you on the path toward becoming a Resilience Ready Leader. Engage your team to inspire team resilience.

Step 1. Practice Empathy

Take Action

- Complete an emotional intelligence assessment — An emotional intelligence assessment will help you to become more self-aware across the four domains of emotional intelligence — self-awareness, self-management, social awareness, and relationship management. Your feedback will include recommendations on how to more effectively interact and communicate with others.
- Listen more, talk less — Become better skilled at reflective listening, where you reflect on what someone else is saying by repeating, summarizing, or paraphrasing what you hear the other person say.

Inspiring Team Resilience Discussion Questions

Take Action

- Download the Inspiring Team Resilience — Partnership Discussion Questions and schedule discussions with your team. Visit https://ResilienceReady.today.

Resources

You may wish to use the accompanying *Resilience Ready Leader's Guide* workbook to complete these exercises. Additional resources also are available at https://ResilienceReady.today.

If you could use support with assessments and taking action, contact me at vivian@vivianblade.com.

Chapter 9

Praise

RESILIENCE READY PRINCIPLE 5

"I have always believed that the way you treat your employees is the way they will treat your customers, and that people flourish when they are praised."
— Sir Richard Branson

"Develop an attitude of gratitude. Say thank you to everyone you meet for everything they do for you." — Brian Tracy

Elizabeth smiled as she opened the envelope and began to read the note inside. It was from her boss, Veronica. "Elizabeth was asked to lead the crisis management team for their department, on top of her regular day-to-day responsibilities, of course," Tim explains. "She only had a couple of days to pull together the team kickoff meeting, which went very well in getting the project scope defined and sub-teams identified. Elizabeth was pleasantly surprised to receive the note. She didn't think Veronica had noticed this small accomplishment, since it was simply what needed to be done to get the project started. But Veronica knew the extra effort Elizabeth had put in to get this done and wanted to make sure she knew it hadn't gone unnoticed.

"Later that afternoon, Veronica stopped by Elizabeth's office to reinforce her appreciation and recognition for her effort. Elizabeth later shared with me how much she appreciated that Veronica took the time to recognize her. She had proudly placed the note on her desk. Her spirit was uplifted during a time that seemed so chaotic, overwhelming, and stressful. She continued to do a great job leading this team!"

Why Praise Is Important to Achieving Resilience

It's easy to focus on what is *not* going well during a crisis. Praise sets aside time to look back and reflect on not only the struggles, but also the progress and how far you've come along the way. Praise is an acknowledgement of appreciation and recognition and demonstrates that "I see you!"; "I appreciate you!"; and "We'll get through this together!" Praise says that I am grateful for this time, even though it's difficult, and grateful for the people with whom I'm going through it. Praise recognizes both the *effort* and *progress* of getting through the struggle.

Praise is an acknowledgement of appreciation and recognition and demonstrates that "I see you!"; "I appreciate you!"; and "We'll get through this together!" #ResilienceReady

Praise is not only outwardly focused to others, but also provides opportunity for self-reflection, self-recognition, and self-appreciation. Praise infuses a sense of gratitude, not pride. And that gratitude fuels a renewed purpose and energy to keep going. Take the time to celebrate along the journey through the crisis to help maintain a momentum of energy and progress.

How a Crisis Impacts Praise

During a crisis, there's so much work to get done quickly. It can seem like people are running around with their heads cut off. Focus on the work. It's easy to overlook or forget to recognize and praise others, especially if praise is not a strong part of your organization's culture. It may not be intentional, but the pace and volume of work can relegate praise to the back seat.

John Hackett describes how different types of crises have the potential to impact praise, and shares steps he took to alleviate that impact:

"Retail sales are often impacted by significant events such as a competitor store opening nearby, a store remodel, or a natural disaster like a hurricane or snowstorm. Too frequently, employees may work their hardest during a crisis and be rewarded the least because rewards are largely based on sales or profits. I tried to send a letter to every store manager every year after results were in. Even if they had a bad financial year, I found other accomplishments to praise them about and recognize them on."

The level of challenge can make you feel defeated. If you don't ever take the time to recognize progress, the sense of defeat increases, which depletes energy. On the contrary, praise fuels energy.

Recognition can seem one-sided with the people working most closely with you. You may privately or publicly recognize those individuals with whose work you are most familiar. This makes others feel like they are not valued, or even invisible.

During a crisis, there are so many opportunities for praise you don't even have to look hard to find them. You just have to be aware of all the effort and progress taking place around you, and be generous with "thank yous", pats on the back, and, in some cases, tangible rewards.

Consequences When Praise Is Lacking

Praise is not a part of some organizational cultures. Their philosophy is, "Employees are doing their job. Isn't their paycheck enough?"

I recall talking with a friend who had just left his job. About two years prior he had taken a role as a branch manager for a regional bank. After months of extra effort to open the branch, hire and train staff, and build the customer base to one of the fastest growing branches in the company, he felt unfulfilled. Even though he had built relationships with his customers, it seemed that all the company really cared about were the numbers; whether or not the branch made their goals. He was disappointed that neither his regional manager nor anyone from corporate recognized his team's hard work and progress. It was difficult to keep up morale when they were constantly under pressure and being criticized. He decided to leave that job and look for an opportunity at an organization with a more positive culture.

You want people to be invested. Success in achieving your organization's objectives won't happen unless employees give more than the base-level expectations. Sure, people don't just work for the glory. But Maslow demonstrated in the hierarchy of needs that people need acceptance, recognition, and accomplishment to achieve personal fulfillment.

Gallup's engagement research finds that organizational cultures lacking employee recognition are more common than you might expect. When employees' work and accomplishments are not recognized, they don't feel valued or appreciated, leading to lower levels of engagement and commitment and higher levels of employee turnover. Gallup further reports that employees who don't feel adequate recognition are twice as likely to leave within the next year.

When praise and appreciation are lacking, there's little basis for employees to feel that you even notice them, value them, or genuinely care about them or their well-being. Individuals and teams stuck in the Victim and Settled Stages are absent of praise. The work environment becomes aggressive, with employees competing for attention. This can result in diminished productivity and collaboration, and weakened operating results.

Consider This

When you have been in a work environment where appreciation or recognition were *not* often expressed, how did that personally affect you?

Advantages of a Strong Praise Culture

During a crisis, most employees are putting in long hours, taking on extra responsibilities, and doing whatever it takes to get from treading water to swimming through the waves. Think about the times you've accomplished something and someone called attention to it. Didn't that help keep you going?

I remember the many games during my son's basketball career, from preschool through college, where the games ended in a tie, taking them into overtime. The difference in how the team played through the overtime had a lot to do with how the coach engaged with the team beyond just drawing up the plays. If the coach was yelling in anger at the smallest mistakes, players shut down. If the coach clapped his hands as the team executed their plays and coached constructively through the mistakes, the team was fired up and somehow found the energy to fight hard for a victory, tired legs, lungs, and all.

When others recognize your work and accomplishments, you feel valued and appreciated. You're willing to give even greater effort. As leader, you are in the best position to do the same for your team. When recognition is present, employees feel better about their work environment. Teamwork and collaboration increase, which is much needed during these times. Engagement and commitment increase as well. Praise also is a form of feedback. Given the volume and pace of work, constructive feedback helps employees know how they are doing. Constructive feedback must go beyond "what you can do better" to include "what you're doing well."

When recognition is present, employees feel better about their work environment. #ResilienceReady

Consider This

When you have been in a work environment where appreciation and recognition were frequently expressed, how did that personally affect you?

Steps to Becoming Resilience Ready

Steps to Develop a Habit of Praise

Getting into a habit of practicing gratitude and praise will positively influence your perspective, sense of hopefulness, and faith. This helps you to be more present to what is going on around you in the moment, and to be intentional about finding the positive in the midst of chaos and fear. Resilient leaders take time to extend praise on three levels:

- Step 1. Practice ***gratitude***
- Step 2. Show ***self-love and appreciation***
- Step 3. Generously ***appreciate and recognize others***

Step 1. Practice Gratitude

As the COVID-19 virus spread around the world, daily life as we knew it quickly began to change. I delivered a professional development workshop at a conference the week that governors from a number of states began issuing shelter-at-home orders. Employers were asking employees to work from home. Large gatherings were cancelled. Schools would soon be closed to in-person classes. Businesses were closing — restaurants, salons, retail stores. The pandemic was spreading quickly. There were no treatments or vaccines. People of all ages were getting the virus. People were dying by the thousands. Federal, state, and local officials were trying to determine the best course of action to minimize the damage. We were fighting a war against an invisible enemy, and without everyone enacting drastic measures, the impact was projected to take as many as hundreds of thousands of lives.

The news was grim and pervasive. People were anxious and stressed. They didn't know how they would survive financially with the economy shut down. It was like mayhem everywhere. It was as if we were living through the most frightening horror movie. The effect of the dire news was causing me anxiety.

One day during the crisis, I was talking with Raymond Gazaway, an entrepreneur, friend, and mentor, about the seriousness of the situation. We turned our attention toward the window. The beauty of spring was beginning to unfold. We looked at the trees budding and flowers blooming. Though we had seen them before, we hadn't viewed them with the same sense of gratitude for their beauty and existence. He reminded me that in our living and breathing, we could take in the sights, sounds, and smells of each season, and find gratitude in our presence among them. In spite of the loss and everything going on around us, we were still here and still had a chance to live purposefully, even if what we were about to go through might be extremely difficult.

In a crisis especially, you need a space within yourself where you can find peace. Gratitude can help you find that space. It's so easy to get caught up in the fear and negativity that come with a crisis. A lot of times your first instinct might be to blame a higher power for the events. You can't understand how God could allow bad things to happen. You may feel that God doesn't care, that He's not present or doesn't hear you. Though there is chaos around you, your human existence is a gift, and you can find a glimpse of hope for a brighter future if you look for it.

A practice of gratitude can help you find a ray of light in your darkest moments. You may use a few minutes upon waking in the morning or before bed in the evening for meditation and reflection. You may step outside to breathe the fresh air and enjoy the beauty of nature around you. Find a time when you can be still and block out the chaos for even a few minutes. In my life, my faith in God and prayer help keep me grateful and hopeful. My power and my strength come from my faith.

Ask yourself, "What am I personally thankful for at this time?" You might consider giving gratitude for:

- What went well today
- Another day of life and health for you, your family, your friends, and your team
- The warmth of the sun and the beauty around you
- The people you work with, those you have the opportunity to invest in and support.

Reconnect with your personal core values and with practices that restore peace and hope. As heavy as the load may be, a reminder that God is still there seeing me through the storm uplifts my spirit. I can honor Him by giving Him my attention, gratitude, and praise.

Jeremiah 29:11 reminds us: "'For I know the plans I have for you,' declares the LORD, 'plans to prosper you and not to harm you, plans to give you hope and a future.'"

Consider This

In what ways do you practice gratitude? How have you seen gratitude make a difference for yourself and others?

Step 2. Show Self-Love and Appreciation

You may not think to praise yourself for your resilience in getting through the crisis. You're usually hardest on yourself, with a lot of negative self-talk about what is going wrong or your incapability getting in the way. We all make mistakes. Not every decision or action will come out perfect. Give yourself some grace, not expecting that you have to be perfect at everything or have all the answers. You may not believe you're worthy. You may believe only the big accomplishments are worth recognizing. Give yourself credit for the effort and the small milestones you accomplish, even when everything doesn't go exactly as planned.

Appreciating yourself can also be uncomfortable. Be generous to yourself. Self-love is crucial. If you don't love and respect yourself, you can't care for others. Jesus Christ's love for mankind is an example of how to love yourself and others.

If you don't love and respect yourself, you can't care for others. #ResilienceReady

---

Self-love and appreciation don't have to be self-serving or all about what you yourself have done. Your greatest reward is in what you have done to help others, and in the collective efforts in working together with others. Pat yourself on the back for what you've accomplished in your work, for your team, and for your community.

In what areas can you extend self-love and appreciation?

- Who were you able to invest in today?
- What difference did you make in someone else's life?
- What did you do to make someone smile?
- Did you give your best effort today?
- What small milestones have you accomplished?
- What contributions did you make to the team's progress?

Step 3. Generously Appreciate & Recognize Others

Praise is a gift that gives back when you give it away. Be generous with appreciating and recognizing others who are going through the crisis with you, and those who play supporting roles. You can look for praise opportunities in the following areas:

Praise for Their Sacrifices

- Share your appreciation with your family, your immediate circle, and your team for the sacrifices they're making. You may be working long hours and your family has to take on extra responsibilities at home. Your lack of presence alone is a void. Your team is sacrificing their personal lives and even their regular job responsibilities in order to pitch in and help during the crisis. People are absorbing more than normal during these times. Their families, as a result, are sacrificing as well.
- As is the case with natural disasters, the COVID-19 pandemic, or September 11, extend praise to everyone on the frontlines of the crisis for their sacrifices and accomplishments. People in these roles are usually at greatest risk and often more

overwhelmed than others. They are the most vulnerable and often the least appreciated.

Praise for Their Effort and Success

- Acknowledge and say thank you for the effort people are putting in to make it all work. People are going above and beyond, making personal sacrifices for the sake of the team. You often don't see what a person's sacrifices are. You can take it for granted as "part of the job," and with remote teams even less of the effort is visible.
- Praise the small accomplishments which often take a lot of effort. Those small accomplishments add up to big progress toward your goals.
- Praise your team members for how they juggle all their balls in the air, and for the work they are doing together.

Praise is a gift that gives back when you give it away. #ResilienceReady

---

Best Practices for Team Appreciation & Recognition

Following are several types of appreciation and recognition preferred by the most engaged employees:

- Personalization — Everyone is different and likely has a preference in how they want to be recognized. Make praise personalized to the individual by asking their preference. Do they want to be recognized publicly or privately? What tokens of appreciation or rewards might they like best? Recognition does not have to be expensive or elaborate, and should include options, in addition to monetary rewards.

  During one-on-one meetings with my team members, I would ask each person individually how they would like to be recognized, and I ensured to plan and follow through accordingly. Some team members like their accomplishments mentioned during team meetings, while others prefer the recognition with a stop by their office or a special note. I made it a point to share the accomplishments of various individuals with my boss. These types of recognition are requested much more frequently than gifts or monetary rewards.

- Say "Thank you" — The simplicity of recognition can be the most powerful. A simple "thank you" is a good start. Though a hand-written note or card is nice from time to time, saying "thank you" in the moment can have even more impact. Recognition from a senior leader or CEO is especially significant and memorable.
- Timely and specific — Just as is recommended with any employee feedback, make praise timely around the occurrence or accomplishment which you are recognizing. And be specific about what the recognition is for, which helps to communicate your attentiveness and reinforces the behaviors aligned with organizational values across the team.
- Paid time off — Employees appreciate extra PTO. Some may use the extra time for personal use with family, for travel, or for much-needed rest and relaxation. Many employees volunteer their time with non-profit organizations and would welcome the extra PTO to give back. Time off, or donating your extra time to focus on meaningful causes and endeavors, rejuvenates your energy physically, emotionally, and spiritually. Some organizations look upon people who take PTO as less committed. Productivity weakens when the human mind and body are tired and worn down. A crisis can easily take a person into that state.
- Engage the team — Encourage team members to practice praise in each of the three areas — practice gratitude, show self-love and appreciation, and generously acknowledge and recognize others. Build a practice around praise and recognition within your team culture. As you model praise, others will recognize its importance, acceptance, and impact. Provide space for team members to share their gratitude and to recognize each other. Engage your team in brainstorming ideas for how they would like to make recognition a standard daily practice.

Jerry, a leader with a former client of mine, implemented "Thank You Thursdays" with his team. They created a brief form on their intranet where team members can post brief yet meaningful recognition for their colleagues. Jerry allocates time on the agenda for team members to share the prior week's recognition submissions during their Thursday team meetings. Jerry says that you can feel the pride, appreciation for being acknowledged, and team cohesion that has resulted from this small act. These recognitions also are included in employees' performance management records.

Consider This

I am a member of the part-time faculty of the University of Louisville College of Business. In this email to faculty and staff (reprinted with permission), Dean Todd Mooradian exemplifies generous appreciation and recognition of others.

From: Mooradian, Todd

Subject: Tuesday thought — let's not forget what extraordinary things we're doing

It's a Tuesday in the middle of July and the middle of the pandemic and I think the "new normal" is starting to feel normal — and we should not let anything desensitize us to the truly wondrous and wonderful things we are doing and others are doing all around us all the time.

We're all starting to get used to remote work and to being apart. I think we're becoming habituated to feeling swamped by the amount of information we could read and study about this virus, if only we had time. We're becoming hardened to the stress of changing trends and conflicting data. I know that the uncertainty of the pandemic and of preparing for the start of a school year like no school year before it have long ago passed "overwhelming."

This morning something made me think about the fact that we cannot let these times or this virus make us unappreciative of the remarkable things people all around us are doing — the things we ourselves are doing in the face of real and substantial challenges. We cannot let the extraordinary become so ordinary that we don't recognize it and celebrate it.

I think the College of Business community is doing an unbelievable job enduring these challenges and preparing to be great against any standard — not just "considering the pandemic" — when the fall semester begins in three weeks. THANK YOU!!! Thank you for rising to meet this test. Thank you — our staff, our faculty, our students, and our partners; all of you — for caring so committedly and so passionately about the quality of our programs, our services, our classes, and our community. Thank you for remembering every day to care about one another as friends and to invest, when we can, in good cheer and fellowship — even good humor as we make our way.

We have gone beyond what we thought was our "best;" every week, every day, and every hour I am seeing people throughout our college digging deep and doing whatever is required, and it is an amazing thing. You're great! And we're all going to be great when the school year starts next month.

Happy Tuesday.
Todd

Todd A. Mooradian, PhD | Dean
University of Louisville, College of Business

It's Time to Lead with Praise!

To ensure praise doesn't get overlooked, add it to your to-do list so that you see it as an action item and plan time for it each day. If you take the time to look, you'll find ample opportunity to praise in each of the three ways that other resilient leaders practice.

Praise can take only a second to share, but the impact is infinite! Praise demonstrates that "I see you!" and "We'll get through this together!"

Remember:

- → Praise is an acknowledgement of appreciation and recognition and demonstrates that "I see you!"; "I appreciate you!"; and "We'll get through this together!"
- → Praise is not only outward-focused to others, but also provides opportunity for self-reflection, self-recognition, and self-appreciation.
- → When others recognize your work and accomplishments, you feel valued and appreciated. You're willing to give even greater effort. As leader, you are in the best position to do the same for your team.
- → Getting into a habit of practicing gratitude and praise will positively influence your perspective, sense of hopefulness, and faith.
- → Resilient leaders take time to extend praise on three levels:
  - Step 1. Practice gratitude — though there is chaos around you, your human existence is a gift, and you can find a glimpse of hope for a brighter future if you look for it.
  - Step 2. Show self-love and appreciation — pat yourself on the back for what you've accomplished in your work, for your team, and for your community.
  - Step 3. Generously appreciate and recognize others — for the effort put forth and their accomplishments.
- → Be generous, appreciating and recognizing others going through the crisis with you, and those playing supporting roles.

Resilience Ready Today

Rapid Start Activity

PRINCIPLE 5. PRAISE

Goal: Enhance personal value and self-worth through generously extending gratitude and recognition to self and others.

Following are the most immediate reflections or actions that will get you on the path toward becoming a Resilience Ready Leader. Engage your team to inspire team resilience.

Step 3. Generously Appreciate & Recognize Others

Take Action

- In what ways did you extend praise to someone else today? Were there potential opportunities you missed?
- Share your best ideas for recognizing others at https://ResilienceReady.today/praise.

Inspiring Team Resilience Discussion Questions

Take Action

- Download the Inspiring Team Resilience — Praise Discussion Questions and schedule time to have discussions with your team. Visit https://ResilienceReady.today.

Resources

You may wish to use the accompanying *Resilience Ready Leader's Guide* workbook to complete these exercises. Additional resources also are available at https://ResilienceReady.today.

If you could use support with assessments and in taking action, contact me at vivian@vivianblade.com.

Chapter 10

Are You Resilience Ready?

"In a crisis, be aware of the danger–but recognize the opportunity." — John F. Kennedy

"Well, we made it through this component supplier issue in one piece. Actually, better than one piece," Tim shares proudly. "Our team was able to pull off an amazing recovery. We were able to ramp up production with two additional component suppliers in a matter of days, one which we also had to qualify first. Though somewhat delayed, we were able to rebuild a supply of incoming components to fill our orders. And, we were able to launch two new services to provide customer maintenance and reduce some of their procurement costs. I remember when this all started. We didn't think we'd be able to recover so quickly and feared losing our shirts from this.

"As I thought about what made the difference, I'd first have to say the leadership team came together, stopped placing blame, and decided to partner to make it work. We stopped being victims, focusing on what we *couldn't* do, and instead kept focused on our commitment to doing everything we possibly could to serve our customers well. Our customers were depending on us! We pulled in our teams to brainstorm and implement new ideas. They had to know we believed in them. We removed a lot of the bureaucracy, and eliminated the phrases, 'that will never work' and 'we've always done it this way' from our vocabulary.

"Everybody was working extremely hard. Some employees took on the extra responsibilities of being on one of the many recovery teams. Those teams did a great job of mapping out what needed to be done, corralling the resources, and remaining agile as conditions changed. It was tiring and stressful, to say the least. There was this energy that developed from working together to solve a big problem. Our teams love a good challenge!

"Oh, yes, the rumors were flying around. We did a lot of communicating to ensure everyone was well informed. We needed to maintain transparency and strengthen trust. We couldn't afford for employee morale to be low. Leaders did a lot of checking in with people, had group conversations about what was going on, and provided resources for dealing with anxiety and stress. It was important for leaders to recognize all the extra effort everyone was putting in. Even a simple 'thank you' was important to frequently say.

"At this stage, I'd say the accomplishment from having tackled this crisis and getting our customers what they need has us thriving. We had one big celebration with lots of food, awards, and praise for a job well done. We learned a lot through this process. To get through this, we needed more than a crisis management plan. Our success has been all about the people on our team making it happen. How we worked together, treated each other, and supported each other through this was key. Getting back to our core values and staying focused on our purpose were instrumental.

"Looking back, I'd say we were pretty resilient. Our experience going through this has made us more resilient individuals, more resilient teams, and a more resilient organization... even better prepared for the next crisis, which, by the way, is already here! We'll talk about that another day."

Are You Resilience Ready?

A crisis doesn't wait until you're ready and doesn't come on your terms. Getting through a crisis is not easy. You have to decide that you are ready to stop being a victim, get in the driver's seat, and move ahead through the chaotic intersections you frequently come to during a crisis. You have a choice at these intersections. Will you remain in the Victim Stage? Or, will you take a deep breath and take full responsibility for persevering through in order to thrive? Are you *Resilience Ready*?

Personal resilience must be discovered before you can inspire resilience in your team or organization. You may call yourself 'resilient', but if truly undeveloped, people will see through the facade when your fear and lack of confidence undeniably show through. Becoming Resilience Ready is a process that begins with understanding, adopting, and putting the Resilience Ready Principles into practice day-to-day. These principles become core to who you are and second nature to how you live and how you lead.

Resilience develops and strengthens from being tested. #ResilienceReady

But that's not enough. Resilience develops and strengthens from being tested, similar to how your muscles strengthen from the resistance when you lift weights. The heavier and more challenging the weight, the more your muscles have the opportunity to develop. The heavier and more challenging the resistance you experience in a crisis, the more your resilience has the opportunity to develop. You have to go through the fire. However, how you respond to that opportunity for growth will determine whether you fall from or rise to the crisis. Respond as a victim, settling for your condition or surviving as you barely get by, and you risk a pretty hard fall. You risk continuing to exist as a survivor. Rising from the crisis occurs when you find the fortitude and courage deep inside to push through with intention, using the Resilience Ready Principles as your roadmap.

Rising from the crisis occurs when you find the fortitude and courage deep inside to push through with intention, using the Resilience Ready Principles as your roadmap. #ResilienceReady

Finding resilience for yourself and being able to bridge that resilience into how you lead is powerful. When you are Resilience Ready and apply the Resilience Ready Principles in your leadership, the overwhelm that easily escalates with a crisis will subside not only for you, but for your team and your organization. Recovery from a disruption will occur more quickly, enabling you to achieve faster results.

Finding resilience for yourself and being able to bridge that resilience into how you lead is powerful. #ResilienceReady

What puts you in the best position to *thrive* as you go through and emerge from a crisis? The *combined* approach of having an operational crisis management plan in place and executing that plan in a culture that elevates your human capital through a *resilience inspired servant leadership practice*.

The Resilience Ready framework I've shared with you in this book equips you to build that type of resilience inspired servant leadership culture.

It's Time To Lead With Resilience!

Where Do You Go From Here?

Are you ready to stop just surviving a crisis? Are you ready to begin thriving? It's time to take action. It's time to become Resilience Ready. Here's how...

Inspiring Personal Resilience

The road to becoming Resilience Ready requires your awareness, intention, and commitment to the ongoing work. You'll also need to give yourself some grace for the imperfection you'll experience as you learn, practice, and adapt these principles to any given crisis you encounter.

The following steps will guide you in becoming *Resilience Ready*, free from being stuck in the Victim Stage to living and leading in the Thriving Stage:

1. Grasp the principles

This book has taken you in-depth on each of the five Resilience Ready Principles. Study, review, and understand the principles and associated leadership practices to begin developing your resilience skill. Reference the *Consider This* exercises in each chapter and the *Deepen Your Readiness* exercises in the accompanying *Resilience Ready Leader's Guide* workbook to assist you.

2. Identify and address the obstacles to becoming Resilience Ready

Your next focus is to identify, prioritize, and address the specific obstacles to deepening your personal resilience skill. Resilience is a developed skill that begins at an individual level, and collectively can grow into a strength of team and organizational resilience.

Revisit *Chapter 3. Why Are Leaders Failing at Resilience* to evaluate the obstacles threatening your personal capacity to lead with resilience. Prioritize the obstacles contributing the most serious threats to your personal resilience capacity. Focus on eliminating the most pressing obstacles first.

- *The walls of fear*: The barriers that keep you stuck in fear and stress.
    - Wall 1. Fear of uncertainty
    - Wall 2. Fear of loss
    - Wall 3. Fear of failure

Which of the three walls of fear are barriers to your personal ability to become a Resilience Ready Leader?

Name the types of fears you are experiencing. Identify how those fears manifest internally, influencing your behavioral and emotional response.

- *Your internal crisis*: Five stages of internal crisis response

Review the five stages of internal crisis response and take the Resilience Ready Self-Assessment to determine where you currently are in your resilience readiness and what may be contributing factors. The Resilience Ready Feedback Survey is also a good resource for getting input from others.

- o Stage 1. Victim Stage
- o Stage 2. Settled Stage
- o Stage 3. Surviving Stage
- o Stage 4. Courageous Stage
- o Stage 5. Thriving Stage

Where are you personally across the five stages? If currently not in crisis, which stage represents your typical response pattern? What is keeping you from reaching the Thriving Stage?

Work on moving your tendency to react in protection mode from your primitive amygdala brain into the prefrontal neocortex area of the brain, where you can more thoughtfully process your emotions, thoughts, and intention toward taking action. This process will enable you and your team to fully engage the Resilience Ready Principles in moving from the Victim Stage to the Thriving Stage.

3. Take action toward becoming Resilience Ready

By addressing your obstacles, you can begin taking steps toward becoming Resilience Ready.

a) *Practice the Resilience Ready Principles* — Identify opportunities to integrate the Resilience Ready Principles into your life and leadership practice. Align your practice of these principles to your personality, values, needs, and leadership style. Engage a mentor or executive coach to help you explore ideas and keep you accountable.

b) Reflect and adjust — Reflect on the outcomes. Was the result what you expected? What would you repeat or do differently next time? Retake the Resilience Ready Self-Assessment to see how your resilience readiness has evolved. Commit to ongoing learning, development, and integration of these principles into your leadership practice.

Tackling Immediate Needs

You may be in a crisis right now and need to quickly ramp up with resilience to help you get through it. What can you do?

Take a moment to close your eyes and reflect on your current crisis. What most concerns you? What gives you that sinking feeling in your stomach? Where are you stuck?

Considering your responses to these questions, which of the five Resilience Ready Principles would most help you get unstuck right now?

- Resilience Ready Principle 1. Perspective
- Resilience Ready Principle 2. Purpose
- Resilience Ready Principle 3. Perseverance
- Resilience Ready Principle 4. Partnership
- Resilience Ready Principle 5. Praise

Let that be your starting point. You don't have to tackle every resilience principle at once, nor do you have to go through them sequentially. Every crisis has its unique set of circumstances. You, your team, and your organization will have different needs during different crises, and you'll be at different maturity levels in your resilience skill.

Always begin by getting a sense of the state of your well-being before you jump into the ring with a crisis. The crisis will win if you are not emotionally ready, and if you are not thoughtfully considering your approach, both personally and as a leader.

Reference the *Consider This* exercises in each chapter and the *Deepen Your Readiness* exercises in the accompanying *Resilience Ready Leader's Guide* workbook to assist you.

Inspiring Team Resilience

As you build your personal resilience skill, you will be able to support and encourage others in building theirs.

1. Be a role model. Lead by the example you would be proud to have others follow.

2. Provide training and support, and create a culture that helps employees build and practice their resilience skills. Revisit *Chapter 3. Why Are Leaders Failing at Resilience* to evaluate the obstacles threatening your team's resilience capacity. Integrate the steps outlined in "Inspiring Personal Resilience" above in working with your team.

3. Gather with your team to complete the *Inspiring Team Resilience* exercises for each principle that you'll find in the *Resilience Ready Leader's Guide* workbook that accompanies this book.

Inspiring Organizational Resilience

Keep in mind that your company's operational crisis management plan needs the complement of a planned, intentional leadership approach for the well-being of your leaders, your teams, and your organization as a whole. A pure focus on operations will leave you vulnerable to uncontrolled fear, panic, and chaos.

1. Your initial focus is to identify and prioritize the specific obstacles that need to be addressed to begin building Resilience Ready Leaders, Resilience Ready Teams, and a Resilience Ready Organization.

Revisit *Chapter 3. Why Are Leaders Failing at Resilience* to evaluate critical gaps organizations face in developing Resilience Ready Leaders. Prioritize the obstacles contributing the most serious threats to your organizational resilience capacity. Focus on addressing the most pressing obstacles first.

- *Critical organizational gaps in developing Resilience Ready Leaders:*
    - Gap 1. Lack of resilience training in leadership development
    - Gap 2. Leadership development is not multidimensional
    - Gap 3. Leadership pipelines are not inclusive

As you dig into each of the three gaps, what are the specific inhibitors your organization must address to make progress toward becoming Resilience Ready?

Once you identify the gaps threatening your organizational capacity to become Resilience Ready, the following steps will guide you through addressing the obstacles.

- o Convene necessary stakeholders to be involved in the process.
- o Prioritize the gaps contributing the most serious threats to your organizational resilience capacity.
- o Take action to address the three gaps. Focus on building a sustainable infrastructure for ongoing development of Resilience Ready Leaders, and growing an organizational culture with a deep resilience skill set.
- o Engage a talent/organizational development expert to guide you in identifying your gaps and determining appropriate actions.

2. Align these resilience principles with the values and competencies important to your organization's success. Define associated behaviors that integrate the principles into the organizational culture.

Resource Support

The exercises in the *Consider This* sections, and the accompanying *Resilience Ready Leader's Guide* workbook, includes resources and activities that can be used individually and as a team as you work through this book and the resilience principles. You'll want to go through the *Deepen Your Readiness* exercises in the workbook to help you work your way through the stages of internal crisis response — from Victim, to Settled, Surviving, Courage, and finally to Thriving — and to address the obstacles identified. You'll find discussion questions you can use to engage your teams in building team and organizational resilience.

Additional resources are available at https://ResilienceReady.today.

If you would like to have a consultation to explore support and solutions to your specific individual or organizational challenges, I am here to help. Simply contact me directly at vivian@vivianblade.com.

My Prayer for You to Thrive

My hope is that leading with resilience inspires and helps you to visualize resilience as a part of your strength. A crisis is such a critical time in your life and in the lives of your families, friends, colleagues, and organizations. I pray that the principles shared in this book help you and those you touch to thrive through the crises you face and beyond.

It's time to lead with resilience!

Are you Resilience Ready?

Review Inquiry

Hey, it's Vivian here.

I hope you've enjoyed the book, finding it both practical and inspiring. I have a favor to ask.

Would you consider giving it a rating wherever you purchased this book? Online bookstores are more likely to promote a book when they feel good about its content, and reader reviews are a great barometer for a book's quality.

So please go to the website where you purchased the book, search for my name and the book title, and leave a review. If able, perhaps consider adding a picture of you holding the book. That increases the likelihood your review will be accepted!

Many thanks in advance,

Vivian Blade

Will You Share the Love?

Get this book for a friend, associate, or family member!

If you have found this book valuable and know others who would find it useful, consider buying them a copy as a gift. Special bulk discounts are available if you would like your whole team or organization to benefit from reading this. Just contact Vivian at vivian@vivianblade.com.

Would You Like Vivian Blade to Speak to Your Organization?

Book Vivian Now!

Vivian accepts a limited number of speaking/coaching/training engagements each year. To learn how you can bring her message to your organization, email Vivian at vivian@vivianblade.com.

Resources

The accompanying ***Resilience Ready Leader's Guide* workbook** is a useful resource for working through the *Consider This, Resilience Ready Rapid Start*, and other activities for each of the Resilience Ready Principles. The workbook is available on Amazon. Contact Vivian at vivian@vivianblade.com to inquire about volume discounts.

Inspiring Team Resilience

Download the "**Inspiring Team Resilience Discussion Questions"** for each of the five Resilience Ready Principles at https://ResilienceReady.today.

Additional Resilience Ready resources for personal, team, and organizational resilience development are available for download at https://ResilienceReady.today.

Bibliography

Chapter 1

Rivera, Kristin, Dave Stainback, PwC Global Crisis Survey 2019, *Crisis Preparedness as the next competitive advantage: Learning from 4,500 crises*, www.pwc.com/globalcrisissurvey

Center on the Developing Child at Harvard University, *What is Resilience?* 2020, https://developingchild.harvard.edu/science/key-concepts/resilience/

Deloitte and Forbes Insights, *A Crisis of Confidence*, 2016, https://www2.deloitte.com/content/dam/Deloitte/us/Documents/risk/us-aers-global-cm-survey-report.pdf

Chapter 2

Bersin, Josh, *Future of Work: The People Imperative Report*, October 2017, Deloitte

Dai, Guangrong, Bryan Ackermann, Korn Ferry, *Are Firms Flunking Stress Tests?*, https://www.kornferry.com/insights/articles/workplace-stress-rising-employee-engagement

Deloitte, *Leading the Social Enterprise: Reinvent with a Human Focus*, 2019 Deloitte Global Human Capital Trends, https://www2.deloitte.com/content/dam/insights/us/articles/5136_HC-Trends-2019/DI_HC-Trends-2019.pdf

Gandhi, Vipula and Jennifer Robison, Gallup, *Business Suffers When Your Employees Do*, August 18, 2020, https://www.gallup.com/workplace/317348/business-suffers-employees.aspx

Chapter 3

Bonnstetter, Bill J., Judy I. Suiter, *The Universal Language DISC Reference Manual*, TTI Success Insights, 1993 – 2018

Brown, Brene', *Dare to Lead*, Penguin Random House, 2018

Deloitte, *Leading the Social Enterprise: Reinvent with a Human Focus*, 2019 Deloitte Global Human Capital Trends, https://www2.deloitte.com/content/dam/insights/us/articles/5136_HC-Trends-2019/DI_HC-Trends-2019.pdf

Kahneman, Daniel, *Thinking Fast and Slow*, Farrar, Straus and Giroux, 2011

Litaker, Grey, Rick Bell, *By the Numbers: Diversity in the Workplace*, Human Capital Media, June 04, 2019, Workplace.com, https://www.workforce.com/news/by-the-numbers-diversity-in-the-workplace

McKinsey & Company and Lean In, *Women in the Workplace 2019*, https://wiw-report.s3.amazonaws.com/Women_in_the_Workplace_2019.pdf

https://womenintheworkplace.com/#!

McKinsey & Company, *Understanding organizational barriers to a more inclusive workplace*, 2020, https://www.mckinsey.com/business-functions/organization/our-insights/understanding-organizational-barriers-to-a-mor e-inclusive-workplace

Rivera, Kristin, Dave Stainback, PwC Global Crisis Survey 2019, *Crisis Preparedness as the next competitive advantage: Learning from 4,500 crises*, www.pwc.com/globalcrisissurvey

Chapter 4

American Psychological Association, *Building your resilience*, 2012, https://www.apa.org/topics/resilience

Chapter 5

Chowdhury, Madhuleena Roy, BA, *The 3 Best Questionnaires for Measuring Values*, May 18, 2020, PositivePsychology.com, https://positivepsychology.com/values-questionnaire/

Cloud, Psychologist Dr. Henry, *10 Things Successful People Never Do Again,* November 29, 2017, Success Magazine, https://www.success.com/10-things-successful-people-never-do-again/

Davis, Tchiki, Ph.D., *39 Core Values — and How to Live by Them*, July 12, 2018, Psychology Today, https://www.psychologytoday.com/us/blog/click-here-happiness/201807/39-core-values-and-how-live-them

Goleman, Daniel, *Emotional Intelligence*, Bantam Books, 1995

Goleman, Daniel, *Primal Leadership: Realizing the Power of Emotional Intelligence*, Harvard Business School Press, 2002

Kahneman, Daniel, *Thinking Fast and Slow*, Farrar, Straus and Giroux, 2011

Psychology Today, *Big 5 Personality Traits*, https://www.psychologytoday.com/us/basics/big-5-personality-traits

Pavlovich, Lahnee, Head of Research and Writing, *Research Review of Personality and Behavioral Assessments*, Athletic Assessments, https://www.athleteassessments.com/personality-and-behavioral-assessments/

Rivera, Kristen, Dave Stainback, Melanie Butler, Dr. Claudia van den Heuvel, *The human side of crisis: Why your people hold the key to crisis outcomes*, PwC Global Crisis Survey, September 19, 2017, PwC, https://www.pwc.com/gx/en/services/advisory/forensics/global-crisis-survey/the-human-side-of-crisis.html

Stemmle, Connie, *Personal Core Values List: 100 Examples of Values to Live By*, July 9, 2020, Develop Good Habits.com, https://www.developgoodhabits.com/core-values/

The Myers Briggs Foundation, *MBTI® Basics > Extraversion or Introversion*, https://www.myersbriggs.org/my-mbti-personality-type/mbti-basics/extraversion-or-introversion.htm

Chapter 6

Bersin, Josh, *Future of Work: The People Imperative Report*, October 2017, Deloitte

Caminiti, Susan, *AT&T's $1 billion gambit: Retraining nearly half its workforce for jobs of the future,* CNBC.com, March 13, 2018, https://www.cnbc.com/2018/03/13/atts-1-billion-gambit-retraining-nearly-half-its-workforce.html

Lewis, Congressman John, *Together, You Can Redeem the Soul of Our Nation,* July 30, 2020, New York Times, https://www.nytimes.com/2020/07/30/opinion/john-lewis-civil-rights-america.html

Chapter 7

Wang, Yanan, *Peak perseverance: Climber reaches Everest summit using prosthetic*, May 20, 2016, Washington Post, Boston Globe, https://www.bostonglobe.com/news/nation/2016/05/20/first-combat-amputee-climbs-everest/7X2goVOplwpkd8uQWPc7zJ/story.html

Chapter 8

Dorsey, Moira; Temkin, Bruce; and Segall, David, *ROI of Customer Experience, 2019*, Qualtrics XM Institute Q2 2019 Consumer Benchmark Study, December 19, 2019, https://www.xminstitute.com/research/2019-roi-cx/

Edelman, *2019 Edelman Trust Barometer Global Report*, https://www.edelman.com/sites/g/files/aatuss191/files/2019-02/2019_Edelman_Trust_Barometer_Global_Report.pdf

Edelman, *2020 Edelman Trust Barometer*, January 19, 2020, https://www.edelman.com/trustbarometer

Edelman, *Edelman Trust Barometer 2020 Global Report*, January 2020, https://www.edelman.com/sites/g/files/aatuss191/files/2020-01/2020%20Edelman%20Trust%20Barometer%20Global%20Report.pdf

Edelman, Richard, *The Evolution of Trust*, January 19, 2020, https://www.edelman.com/research/evolution-trust

Gallup, *State of the American Workplace*, 2017 https://www.gallup.com/workplace/238085/state-american-workplace-report-2017.aspx

Gallup, *What Is Employee Engagement and How Do You Improve It?,* Gallup Q^{12} Employee Engagement Survey, https://www.gallup.com/workplace/285674/improve-employee-engagement-workplace.aspx

Great Place to Work, *Defining the World's Best Workplaces*, 2019, [https://www.greatplacetowork.com/best-workplaces-international/world-s-best-workplaces/2019

Harter, Jim, *4 Factors Driving Record-High Employee Engagement in U.S.,* February 4, 2020, Gallup, https://www.gallup.com/workplace/284180/factors-driving-record-high-employee-engagement.aspx

McKinsey & Company, *Diversity Wins*, 2019 https://www.mckinsey.com/featured-insights/diversity-and-inclusion/diversity-wins-how-inclusion-matters

Metro Louisville / Jefferson County, KY, *Louisville Resilience Strategy Release*, https://louisvilleky.gov/government/resilience-and-community-services/louisville-resilience-strategy-release

Myers, Joe, *Why don't employees trust their bosses?,* World Economic Forum, April 12, 2016, https://www.weforum.org/agenda/2016/04/why-dont-employees-trust-their-bosses/

Shook, Ellyn and Sweet, Julie Accenture, *The Hidden Value of Culture Makers*, https://www.accenture.com/us-en/about/inclusion-diversity/_acnmedia/Thought-Leadership-Assets/PDF-2/Accenture-Getting-To-Equal-2020-Research-Report.pdf

Smith, M. K. (2005). 'Bruce W. Tuckman – forming, storming, norming and performing in groups, *the encyclopaedia of informal education,* https://webspace.science.uu.nl/~daeme101/infed.org-Bruce_W_Tuckman__forming_storming_norming_and_performing_in_groups.pdf

Society for Human Resource Management, *Introduction to the Human Resources Discipline of Diversity*, July 21, 2020 https://www.shrm.org/resourcesandtools/tools-and-samples/toolkits/pages/introdiversity.aspx

Stein, Judith, *Using the Stages of Team Development*, Massachusetts Institute of Technology https://hr.mit.edu/learning-topics/teams/articles/stages-development

The Rockefeller Foundation, *100 Resilient Cities*, https://www.rockefellerfoundation.org/100-resilient-cities/

Chapter 9

Mann, Annamarie and Dvorak, Nate, *Employee Recognition: Low Cost, High Impact*, Gallup.com, June 28, 2016, https://www.gallup.com/workplace/236441/employee-recognition-low-cost-high-impact.aspx

About the Author

Vivian Hairston Blade, MBA, MBB, PMP is a recognized leadership expert and thought leader. She works with the world's top brands, equipping leaders with the resilience that inspires teams to recover quickly in the face of ongoing disruption, and thrive in spite of insurmountable odds. Her impact is felt as a frequent speaker for association conferences, and in delivering transformative leadership development programs, executive coaching, and corporate consulting.

In the face of her own crisis following a successful 20-year corporate career with Fortune 100 companies Humana and GE, Vivian launched her current leadership consulting practice, applying her extensive business, finance, and leadership experience to coach and develop aspiring and established leaders in building high-performance, high-quality, and high-service level organizations. She also works in academia as adjunct faculty at the University of Louisville College of Business.

Vivian is the author of two books, *FuelForward: Discover Proven Practices to Fuel Your Career Forward,* which reveals the unwritten rules to career success, and *Resilience Ready: The Leader's Guide to Thriving Through Unrelenting Crises*. She is a contributor to two books published by the Association for Talent Development *Find Your Fit: A Practical Guide to Landing a Job You'll Love*, and *Work the Problem: How Experts Tackle Workplace Challenges*.

Vivian is also passionate about making a difference in her community, leading and serving on the board of directors for a number of service and professional organizations.

For more information on her inclusive leadership development/talent management consulting, training, assessments, speaking, and executive coaching, contact Vivian at:

vivian@vivianblade.com
502-419-2433
https://vivianblade.com

Connect with Vivian:
https://www.linkedin.com/in/vivianblade/
https://twitter.com/VivianBlade
https://youtube.com/c/VivianBlade

ResilienceReady.today

VivianBlade.com

Made in the USA
Columbia, SC
29 March 2021

34616886R00124